SRA Imagine It!

Challenge
Activities
Blackline Masters

Level 3

Mc Graw Hill **SRA**

Columbus, Ohio

SRAonline.com

 SRA

Printed in the United States of America.

Send all inquiries to this address:
SRA/McGraw-Hill
4400 Easton Commons
Columbus, OH 43219-6188

ISBN: 978-0-07-610362-1
MHID: 0-07-610362-5

3 4 5 6 7 8 9 BCH 13 12 11 10 09 08 07

The McGraw-Hill Companies

Table of Contents

Unit 4 Earth, Moon, and Sun

Unit 5 Communities across Time

6 Unit Storytelling

Name _____ **Date** _____

Phonics

Focus Identifying and pronouncing words with long vowel sounds makes understanding a text easier. When a word ends with a silent e, the vowel before the e often has a long vowel sound.

Examples: twin + e = twine   us + e = use

 **Apply** **Work with a partner. Read the words in the box below.**

whale	**dive**	**huge**
flame	**fire**	**smoke**
late	**time**	**nine**
shape	**cube**	**bite**

On a separate piece of paper, write a paragraph using the words from the list above. Underline all the words in your paragraph that contain a long vowel sound.

Challenge Activities • Phonics

Name _____ Date _____

Antonyms and Synonyms

Focus Thinking of antonyms and synonyms for words makes some sentences easier to understand.

Antonyms are words that mean the opposite or almost the opposite of each other.

Synonyms are words that mean the same or almost the same thing as each other.

Apply **Work with a partner. Decide whether you need to replace the underlined word in the sentences below with a synonym or an antonym. On a separate sheet of paper, write as many antonyms or synonyms as you can think of for each underlined word.**

1. The poor dog was so <u>scared</u> of the fireworks that it hid in the closet.

2. "Yikes! What was that <u>silence</u> I just heard?"

3. The kitten was so <u>gigantic</u> that it fit right into my aunt's hand.

4. The fireworks were <u>quiet</u> and <u>boring</u>.

5. We could see the <u>bright</u> fireworks from miles away.

Rewrite each sentence with the best synonym or antonym. Share your sentences with your partner.

Word Structure • *Challenge Activities*

Name _____ Date _____

Selection Vocabulary

 **Focus** Practicing vocabulary words by using them in sentences can make reading new words easier.

 **Apply** On a separate sheet of paper, write three sentences using the vocabulary words from the box below. Include two vocabulary words in each sentence. Once you use a word, do not use it again.

chores	permission
patient	ignore
especially	grateful
energy	worried

When you are finished, work with a partner to see how many vocabulary words you can use in one sentence. Underline all the vocabulary words in each sentence.

Name _____ Date _____

Cause and Effect

Focus Understanding cause and effect is important to understanding why things happen. An **effect** is *what* happens. The **cause** is *why* something happens.

Apply **Read the poem below. Then, on a separate sheet of paper, identify as many causes and effects in the poem as you can.**

She dropped the egg, and the egg broke on the floor.
She cleaned the egg up and fetched one more.
She carried this egg with the greatest of care.
Oh, no! She tripped. The egg flew in the air!

When you are finished, imagine what some effects would be of an egg flying in the air. Work with a partner to add new lines to the poem. Add at least three more examples of causes and effects. You can choose whether to rhyme or not when adding to the poem.

Name _____ **Date** _____

Spelling

Focus Long vowels sound like their names.

/ā/ spelled a and a_e.　　　/ē/ spelled e and e_e.

/ī/ spelled i and i_e.　　　/ō/ spelled o and o_e.

/ū/ spelled u and u_e.

Apply You are visiting your grandmother. In her attic, you discover an old trunk. You ask your grandmother if you can look inside. She tells you that you can. Write a paragraph about what you find, and use at least ten of the words below in your paragraph. Try to use the challenge words *grateful, patient,* and *poem* in your writing.

tame	wild	choke	wrote	music	fire	blaze	menu
smile	cedar	item	major	cube	complete	total	

Challenge words: poem　patient　grateful

After you have finished writing your paragraph, draw a picture of one thing you found in the trunk. Write a caption for your picture.

Name _____ **Date** _____

Nouns

Copyright © SRA/McGraw-Hill. Permission is granted to reproduce this page for classroom use.

Focus Good readers can identify common and proper nouns in a paragraph.

Common nouns are words that name *general* kinds of people, places, things, or ideas.

Examples: city, plane, dog, girl

Proper nouns are words that name *specific* people, places, things, or ideas.

Examples: New York, Boeing 747, Rover, Lisu Kento

Apply On a separate piece of paper, write a paragraph about one of your favorite authors. Then make two lists, one list of all the common nouns and another list of all the proper nouns in your paragraph.

Trade paragraphs with a partner. On a separate piece of paper, make a list of the common nouns and another list of the proper nouns that you find in your partner's paragraph.

When you are finished, compare lists with your partner. Do you agree with each other's choices of common and proper nouns? If not, explain why.

Name _____ Date _____

Phonics

Focus Remember that the /**j**/ sound can be spelled *ge* and *gi*. The /**s**/ sound can be spelled *ce* and *ci*.

Examples: g<u>i</u>ant, *ju<u>dge</u>*, <u>ce</u>lery, <u>ci</u>ty

The /**ā**/ sound can be spelled *a* and *a_e*. *The /**ē**/ sound can be spelled e and e_e.*

Examples: *ch<u>a</u>nge, gr<u>ape</u>, <u>e</u>ven, h<u>ere</u>*

Apply **Work with a partner and make a list of words with the /j/ sound and the /s/ sound spelled *ge*, *gi*, *ce*, and *ci*. Make another list of words with the /ā/ sound spelled *a_e* and the /ē/ sound spelled *e_e*.**

Write four questions for your partner using some of the words on the list. Trade questions with your partner. Underline the words with the /j/ and /s/ sounds. Circle the words with the /a–/ and /e–/ sounds.

Answer the questions, and explain your answers to your partner.

Name _____ Date _____

Compound Words

Focus

A **compound word** is a word that is formed by adding two separate words together to make a new word.

Examples: fire + fighter = firefighter
ball + park = ballpark

Apply

Write eight compound word problems like the examples in the Focus box above for a partner. Leave one part of your word problem blank. Write your answers to the problems on a separate sheet of paper. Exchange problems with your partner.

When you and your partner have finished solving each other's word equations, compare your answers. Choose one word for which you have different answers. Can you think of even more answers for that word?

Pick one word where your answers are the same. Can you think of more answers for that word?

Word Structure • *Challenge Activities*

Name _____ Date _____

Selection Vocabulary

Focus Readers can figure out what vocabulary words mean by finding context clues in sentences.

Apply On a separate sheet of paper, write a sentence for each vocabulary word from the box below that gives a clue about its meaning. Trade sentences with a partner. Match the clue sentences with the vocabulary words.

curious	miserable
deserted	faith
condition	persuaded
exchange	struggled

When you finish, share the reasons for your answers with your partner.

Name _____ Date _____

Spelling

Focus A **compound word** is a word made of two smaller words joined together.

/**s**/ is found in words where the letter *c* is followed by *e*, *i*, or *y*.

/**j**/ is found in words where the letter *g* is followed by *e*, *i*, or *y*.

Apply You are a newspaper reporter. You have just reached the scene of an accident. Your job is to write a news story for the paper that tells your readers what happened. Write at least two paragraphs, and use at least eight words below in your story. Try to include the challenge words *exchange, garbage,* and *distance* in your writing.

shipwreck	huge	twice	homework	bulldog	gentle	range
city	since	notebook	decent	waterfront	germ	logic	agent

Challenge words: exchange garbage distance

Create a headline for your news story. Be sure it gives readers an idea of what the story is about.

Spelling • *Challenge Activities*

Name _____ Date _____

Verbs and Verb Phrases

Focus Readers should be able to identify verbs and verb phrases in a written passage. Then they can identify verbs and verb phrases in their own writing. **Verbs** express what actions happen in a sentence. Verbs that are more than one word are **verb phrases.**

Apply **Read the paragraph below. On a separate sheet of paper, make a list of the verbs and verb phrases. Discuss your answers with a partner or your teacher.**

Tonio was looking through the car window. The dark sky was filled with stars that twinkled brightly. Tonio's eyes were closing with sleep. When he opened his eyes again, the sky had turned from black to gray. The stars were gone from sight. The first glimmer of a golden sun peeked out. Morning had come.

Then, write a paragraph about something you see outside. It might be the sky, trees, a building, or some children playing. Underline the verbs and the verb phrases in your paragraph.

When you finish, share your paragraph with a partner.

Name _____ Date _____

Phonics

 Readers should be able to identify and use words with the long vowel sounds /**ā**/, /**ē**/, /**ī**/, /**ō**/, and /**ū**/. Readers should also recognize the /**j**/ sound spelled *j* and *_dge* and the /**s**/ sound spelled *s* and *cy*.

 **On a separate sheet of paper, write a word with each sound and spelling from the box below.**

---

the /ā/ sound spelled *a* and *a_e*	the /ē/ sound spelled *e* and *e_e*	the /ī/ sound spelled *i* and *i_e*
the /ō/ sound spelled *o* and *o_e*	the /ū/ sound spelled *u* and *u_e*	the /j/ sound spelled *j* and *_dge*
	the /s/ sound spelled *s* and *cy*	

Write sentences with each word. If you can, use two or three of your words in the same sentence.

When you finish, share your sentences with your family.

Phonics • *Challenge Activities*

Name _____ **Date** _____

Contractions

Focus **Contractions** are a good way to shorten two words into one. The apostrophe (') in a contraction replaces the missing letter or letters in the part of the word that was shortened.

Apply On a separate sheet of paper, list seven contractions that end with *-n't*. Substitute each contraction for the word *don't* in the rhyme below. Then, finish the rhyme by filling in the two words that the contraction stands for.

The wonderful apostrophe: It's hardly bigger than a dot. Yet without this punctuation mark, <u>don't</u> would be

_____ _____.

When you finish, meet with a small group to compare lists. Make a group list of all the different *-n't* contractions you came up with. Can you think of any other contractions with *-n't* to add to the list?

Name _____ Date _____

Selection Vocabulary

Focus Some word clues help readers pronounce words. Other word clues help readers remember how to spell words. Still other word clues help readers remember what words mean.

Apply On a separate sheet of paper, work with a partner to write sentences with two clues about each vocabulary word below. Exchange sentences with another pair of partners. Match the vocabulary words with the clues, and then try to write a paragraph using all the vocabulary words.

foreign enthusiastic	assure peculiar	pastel translation	glum insisted

Vocabulary • *Challenge Activities*

Name _____ Date _____

Author's Point of View

Focus The **author's point of view** is how an author chooses to tell a story.

- When the author is part of the story, the story is being told in **first person point of view.** When using the first person point of view, an author uses the words *I, me,* or *we* to tell the story.

- If an author writes a story in the **third person point of view,** the author would be outside the story using words like *he, she,* and *they.*

Apply On a separate sheet of paper, write a short story about something incredible that you have seen or done. Decide whether you will tell it in the first person or in the third person point of view.

When you finish, make sure your entire story is told from the same point of view.

Trade stories with a partner. What point of view did your partner use? Why do you think your partner chose to use that point of view? Discuss your answers with your partner.

Share your short story with your family.

Challenge Activities • Comprehension Skill

Name _____ Date _____

Spelling

Focus **Contractions** are words formed from two words. Some letters are left out when the two words combine, and an apostrophe takes the place of the missing letters.

/ō/ can be spelled o and o_e.

Apply Jerry decided to study his spelling words by using small wooden blocks with letters on them. When he got up to get a drink, his younger brother rearranged all the letter o's so now they are in the wrong places. In order to continue studying, Jerry needs your help. On another piece of paper, rewrite the words in the box so they are spelled correctly.

haven'ot	wasn'ot	aren'ot	desn'ot	mment
	Challenge words:	'clck	shuldn'ot	

When you are finished, choose at least four of the words, and remove the apostrophes. Include the two challenge words. Trade papers with a partner, and spell the words correctly by adding the missing apostrophes.

Spelling • *Challenge Activities*

Name _____ Date _____

Subject and Predicate

Focus Good readers can identify and change **simple subjects**, **compound subjects**, **simple predicates**, and **compound predicates**.

A **subject** is the person, thing, or idea that a sentence is about.

A **predicate** tells what the subject *is* or what the subject *does*.

Apply Change the subject. Rewrite the following sentences on a separate sheet of paper. If the sentence has a simple subject, change it to a compound subject. If it has a compound subject, change it to a simple subject. Underline all of the simple predicates and circle all of the compound predicates.

1. Rita and Leo built a snow elephant with huge tusks.

2. The chimpanzee skates and rides a tricycle.

3. Franco is an artist.

4. Jarvis practices the drums every day.

5. Sid caught the ball.

6. Rover barked and ran after the squirrel.

7. Jermaine and his family hiked in the mountains.

8. Matt and Carlos wash and dry the dishes.

9. Lila's grandmother shut and locked the door.

10. Mariana walks in the park.

Name _____ **Date** _____

Phonics

Focus Readers need to recognize words with the /ā/ and /ē/ long vowel sounds and **consonant blends.** The /ā/ sound is often spelled *ai_* and *_ay;* /ē/ is often spelled *ee, ea, y,* and *_ie_.* Consonant blends can be at the beginning or at the end of words.

Apply On a separate sheet of paper, make a list of five or more words for each sound or spelling in the box below. Then, make a list of words with consonant blends at the beginning or at the end of the word.

Write two or more paragraphs about something you did last year in school using at least ten of the words you listed.

/ā/ spelled *ai_*	/ā/ spelled *_ay*
/ē/ spelled *ea, ee, _ie_*	/ē/ spelled *y* and *_ey*

When you finish, trade stories with a partner. See if you can find all the words your partner used from his or her list.

Phonics · *Challenge Activities*

Name _____ **Date** _____

Related Words

Focus **Related words** can be grouped together because of a common topic.

Example: A *keyboard,* a *mouse,* and a *screen* are all things found on a computer.

Apply **A word can belong to more than one word topic. What topic does *diamond* belong to in the following group of words?**

diamond   ruby   emerald   _____

What topic does diamond belong to in this group of words?

diamond   pitcher   batter   _____

What topic do these words form?

water   milk   juice   _____

For each word below, make a new topic.

1. water   _____ _____

2. milk   _____ _____

3. juice   _____ _____

Compare answers with a partner. Are your answers different? If they are, how are they different?

Challenge Activities • Word Structure

Name _____ Date _____

Selection Vocabulary

Focus Practicing vocabulary can make both reading and spelling easier. Knowing what words mean and how to spell them is important to using them well.

Apply **Unscramble each vocabulary word below. On a separate sheet of paper, write a sentence using each word.**

1. rdonelsp

2. cryme

3. degish

4. fingmactine

5. glunc

6. lymditi

7. adripse

8. terfedalt

When you finish, work with a partner to write a sentence using at least three of the vocabulary words.

Vocabulary • *Challenge Activities*

Name _____ Date _____

Spelling

Focus

Related words are words that have a similar theme.

/ā/ can be spelled *ai_*, and *_ay*.

/ē/ can be spelled *ea, _y, ee, _ie_,* and *_ey*.

Consonant blends are groups of two or three consonants in which the sound of each letter can be heard.

Apply

Imagine you have just taken a walk on a warm summer's day. You are ready to write an entry in your journal, describing what you saw and did on your walk. On a separate sheet of paper, write your journal entry, using at least ten words from the box below. In your writing, try to use the challenge words *timidly* and *despair*.

mercy	heavy	spray	honey	brief
field	street	alley	plain	turkey
east	day	week	year	claim
	Challenge words: timidly		despair	

Make a sketch at the bottom of your journal entry, showing something you saw on your walk.

Name _____ Date _____

Complete Simple Sentences

Focus Good readers can identify simple sentences. A **simple sentence** has one subject and one predicate. The **subject** of a sentence tells you who or what the sentence is about, and the **predicate** tells you what the subject is or does.

Apply Below are some sayings by Benjamin Franklin. With a partner, decide if the sentences are simple sentences or not. Then, on a separate sheet of paper, work together to explain in writing what each saying means. Underline the simple sentences in your writing.

1. Lost time is never found again.

2. Little strokes fell great oaks.

3. The used key is always bright.

4. The cat in gloves scratches no mice.

5. A sleeping fox catches no poultry.

6. A fool and his money are soon parted.

7. A spoonful of honey will catch more flies than a gallon of vinegar.

8. A true friend is the best possession.

Grammar, Usage, and Mechanics • *Challenge Activities*

Phonics

Focus Readers can improve their spelling by practicing long vowel sounds, consonant sounds, and consonant blends.

Apply Underline the words in the box below with the /ā/, /ē/, /ī/, /ō/, or /ū/ long vowel sounds. Circle the words with the /j/ sound or the /s/ sound. Put boxes around words that begin or end in consonant blends. Remember that some words have more than one of these sounds.

amaze	badge	best	chief	explain
fancy	gentle	giant	here	honey
human	kite	leaves	lonely	pencil
plate	player	speedy	stone	strange

On a separate sheet of paper, write a few paragraphs about an animal. The animal can be real or imaginary. Use at least five of the words in the box in your writing.

Name _____ Date _____

Review of Antonyms, Synonyms, Compound Words, Contractions and Related Words

Focus   Review the meanings of **antonyms** and **synonyms**, **compound words**, **contractions**, and **related words**.

Apply   Find synonyms and antonyms for at least two words in the rhyme below. Write your answers on a separate sheet of paper. Change two words into a contraction. Choose one word from the rhyme, and think of two or more words to make a word family.

The man in the wilderness asked of me,
"How many strawberries grew in the sea?"
I answered him as I had thought good,
"As many as red herrings grow in the wood."

This is a very old rhyme. Do you think it is funny? Why or why not?

Name _____ Date _____

Selection Vocabulary

Focus Practicing vocabulary will help improve how well you read, write, and speak.

Apply **You and a partner are reporters for a newspaper. On a separate sheet of paper, write an article for the paper describing a game you just watched.**

Write about whatever game you want. In your article, try to include all the vocabulary words in the box below.

challenge	compete	equal	leagues
opponents	possess	responded	series

When you finish, gather other articles from your classmates, and create a group newspaper. Share your newspaper with your teacher.

Name _____ Date _____

Main Idea and Supporting Details

Focus Good readers will know the **main idea** and the **supporting details** of a paragraph. The **main idea** is the central thought of the paragraph. The **supporting details** give more information about the main idea in the paragraph.

Apply Choose two of the topics below. On a separate sheet of paper, write a paragraph about each topic you chose. Include supporting details. Give each paragraph a title.

birthdays	summertime	dogs	cats

When you finish, reread your title for each paragraph. Make sure that it matches the main idea.

Comprehension Skill • *Challenge Activities*

Name _____   Date _____

Spelling

Focus

*kn_* at the beginning of a word makes the **/n/** sound.

*wr_* at the beginning of a word makes the **/r/** sound.

ph makes the **/f/** sound.

mb makes the **/m/** sound.

Apply Your good friend Freddy has just done a magic trick for you. Now he wants to know what magic trick you can do. You tell him that you can make the sound of a letter disappear or change by just adding another letter. "Ha!" Freddy says. "That's impossible!" Not only is it possible, you say, but you can do it by adding just an *n*, *r*, *h*, or *m*.

Show Freddy your trick by adding an *n*, *m*, *h*, or an *r* to each of the words in the box below. Write the new words on a separate piece of paper. Underline the silent letter or new sound in each word.

kot	wite	pony	clib	kee
grap	pase	kow	weath	thub
wist	lab	tropy	kife	cob

Challenge words: triump

Name _____ Date _____

Quotation Marks, Commas, and Capitalization

Focus Knowing how to use quotation marks, commas, and capitalization is important to writing what you mean to write. **Quotation marks** report things that people say, **commas** separate important parts of sentences, and **capitalization** is used for proper nouns, titles, and to begin sentences.

Apply Find a paragraph in a book, newspaper, or magazine. Rewrite the paragraph or sentences on a separate sheet of paper. Put in mistakes by taking out some of the capital letters, commas, and quotation marks. Trade paragraphs with a partner. Look for the mistakes in your partner's paragraph and correct them.

Did you find all of your partner's mistakes? Did your partner find all of your mistakes?

Name _____ **Date** _____

/ī/ Sound/Spellings and Consonant Blends

Focus Good readers listen to the sounds of words and then match the sounds with the spellings.

Listen to the /ī/ sound in words spelled *igh, y,* and *ie.*

Listen to the sounds that **consonant blends** make at the beginning and at the end of words.

Apply **Here are some words with the /ī/ sound spelled *igh, y* and *ie,* and words that begin or end with consonant blends. Work with a partner to add at least four words to the list.**

high	fright	light	tight
style	fly	sky	spy
die	lie	pie	tie
grown	last	task	street

On a separate sheet of paper, write four sentences using at least two of the words in each sentence. When you finish, share your sentences with your partner.

Name _____ Date _____

Regular Plurals

Focus There are rules for forming the regular plurals of nouns.

- Add *s* if the noun ends in a consonant or *e.*

- Add -*es* if the noun ends in *x, ch,* or *sh.*

- Change *y* to *i* and add -*es* if the noun ends in *y.*

- Change *f* to *v* and add -*es* if the noun ends in an *f* and makes the *v* sound when it is in its plural form.

Apply **Working with a partner, write each of these words on an index card, one word to a card.**

| berry | flower | butterfly | bird | box | garden | piece | bunny | baby | leaf |

Mix the cards together, and turn them over so you cannot see the words. Take turns picking a card. Look at your word, and write the plural on the back of the card. When you have finished, use some of the words to write a story with your partner.

Read your story to another pair of partners.

Name _____ Date _____

Selection Vocabulary

 Focus The more words readers know, the more fun they can have with them. Word clues and word puzzles are fun to solve.

 Apply **On a separate sheet of paper, use the vocabulary words to make word scramble puzzles. Scramble all of the words in the box below. Trade puzzles with a partner, and solve your partner's puzzles.**

bacteria	dwellers	except	hollow
maze	stored	swarming	

When you have finished, work with your partner to make four new word scramble puzzles. Trade puzzles with another pair of partners, and solve.

Name _____ Date _____

Spelling

Focus For most regular plurals, add -s or -es to the end of the base word.

If the base word ends in:

ch, sh, s, ss, x, z, or *zz*, add -es.

a consonant + -*y*, change the *y* to *i* and add -es.

f, change the *f* to *v,* and add -es.

a vowel + -*y*, just add an -s.

silent -*e*, just add an -s.

/ī/ can be spelled *igh, _y,* and *_ie.*

Apply **You have come to the zoo to study the monkeys. You watch the monkeys for three hours and take notes about what you see. You have to write your notes into a short report.**

Write two or more paragraphs describing what happened and how the monkeys acted while you observed them. Use at least ten words from the box below. Include the challenge words *dwellers* **and** *outcry* **in your report.**

lie	ties	fly	flies	halves	cycles	reply	replies
sigh	monkeys	lunches	fight	knights	spy	spies	
		Challenge words: dwellers		outcry			

Make a cover and illustrate your report. Display your report in the classroom.

Spelling • *Challenge Activities*

Name _____ Date _____

Possessive Nouns and Pronouns

Focus *Whose book is that? Whose footprints are those? Who owns that backpack?* **Possessive nouns** and **possessive pronouns** are important when you read, because they answer questions like these. Remember that possessive pronouns do not need apostrophes.

Apply **Play the *Apostrophe or No Apostrophe* game. Decide if the underlined words need an apostrophe or if the words have an apostrophe that they *do not* need. Rewrite each word correctly on a separate sheet of paper.**

<u>her'</u> coat

<u>puppie's</u> tails

<u>umbrellas</u> handle

<u>families</u> houses

<u>birds</u> beak

<u>books'</u> cover

<u>you'r</u> idea

<u>childrens'</u> game

<u>Toms</u> bike

<u>Thei'r</u> shoes

When you have finished, write a sentence using each correct answer.

Name _____ Date _____

/ō/ Sound/Spellings

Focus The /ō/ **sound** can be spelled in different ways. Two ways are _ow and oa_. The more readers practice pronouncing and spelling words with the /ō/ sound spelled _ow and oa_, the easier it will be to recognize the words when they are reading.

Apply **Find antonyms and synonyms for the words below. Each answer must be a word with the /ō/ sound spelled _ow or oa_. Write your words on a separate sheet of paper.**

Find *antonyms* for

fast   catch   hide   above

Find *synonyms* for

street   ship   get bigger   shine

When you finish, use at least four of the words to write a poem. Share your poem with your family.

Phonics • *Challenge Activities*

Irregular Plurals

Focus Good readers study words that are **irregular plurals** so they can remember them. Irregular plurals are not formed by the same rules as regular plurals.

Apply **Work with a partner. Write each of these words on a different index card.**

deer	sheep	person	mouse
moose	children	goose	teeth

Number the backs of the cards from 1 to 8. Mix the cards up, and then lay them down with the numbers showing. Take turns picking cards. Tell your partner the plural or singular form for each word you pick.

When you finish, divide the cards between you and your partner. On a separate sheet of paper, write two sentences. Make sure you use two words from above in each sentence.

Name _____ Date _____

Selection Vocabulary

Focus Vocabulary words are not just found in books. They are words people use every day.

Apply **A news reporter needs your help. The reporter is very busy and wants you to write a story for him about something that happened today.**

On a separate sheet of paper, write a news report using as many vocabulary words as you can.

beckoned	bringing up	enormous	hatch	responsibility	strange

Oops! No time to hand the reporter your story. You will have to give the report yourself to a partner in your class or to a family member.

Vocabulary • *Challenge Activities*

Name _____ **Date** _____

Fantasy and Reality

Focus In stories that are **fantasy,** the plot has events or characters that would not be found in real life. In stories based on **reality,** the plot has characters and events that could be found in everyday life.

Apply On a separate sheet of paper, write six sentences. Make sure that some of the events in the sentences could happen in reality and that some are fantasy. You can take your sentences from books and magazines, or you can make them up.

When you are done, trade papers with a partner. Identify which sentences are reality and which are fantasy. Talk your answers over with your partner. One hundred years from now, might some of your answers be different?

Name _____ Date _____

Spelling

Copyright © SRA/McGraw-Hill. Permission is granted to reproduce this page for classroom use.

Focus **Irregular plurals** are words that do not add -s or -es to the base word to form a plural.

Some words have the same singular and plural form.   *deer*

Some words change spelling altogether.   *goose, geese*

/ō/ can be spelled _ow and *oa.*

Apply **Your class is having a contest. Find three words in the list below *without* a long vowel sound. Then, decide what is special about those three words. To find the three words, sort all the words by listing them under the categories /ō/, /ī/, /ē/, and *No Long Vowels*. Write your lists on a separate piece of paper.**

toast	mice	women	coach	deer
throw	roast	teeth	crow	oxen
oatmeal	loan	grow	float	fish
	Challenge words: cacti		pillow	

You and another student are tied for first place. To break the tie, your teacher has given you this category: *Irregular Plurals*. Rewrite the category title, and add *all* the plural words on your list that fit the category. Compare lists with a partner to see if you both have the same words.

Spelling • *Challenge Activities*

Name _____ Date _____

Plural Nouns and Irregular Plural Nouns

Focus **Plural nouns** name more than one person, place, or thing. Most plural nouns are regular nouns. There are rules that explain how to form them.

However, there are no rules for forming nouns with **irregular** endings. Good readers just have to study them until they know them.

Apply Fill in each of the boxes with at least three plural nouns. If you need more room, make this chart on another piece of paper.

Nouns with regular endings	Nouns ending in *s*, *ch*, *sh*, *ss*, *z*, *zz*, or *x*	Nouns ending with a consonant and a *y*	Nouns ending with an *f* (change to a *v* in plural)	Nouns with irregular endings

When you have finished, write a story using at least five of the words. Write your story on a separate sheet of paper.

Name _____ **Date** _____

The /ū/ Sound/Spellings

Focus **The /ū/ sound** can be spelled in different ways. Good readers practice pronouncing and writing words with the /ū/ sound spelled _ew and _ue so that they can read them easily.

Apply **Work with a partner. Write these words on index cards—one word on each card.**

few	rescue	nephew	continue
argue	value	barbeque	mew

Turn over the cards so you cannot see the words, and take turns picking cards. After you pick a word, pronounce it, and listen to the /ū/ sound. Then, make up a "clue" question about the word, but do not use the word in your question. For example, suppose you pick the word "fuel." You might ask your partner, "What do you put in a car to make it go?"

When you finish, share your questions with another pair of partners. Are some of your questions different?

Phonics • *Challenge Activities*

Name _____ **Date** _____

Homographs

Focus   **Homographs** are words that are spelled the same but have different meanings. It is important to recognize homographs to make sure that the right word is being used.

Apply   **Here is a list of homographs.**

watch	stick	sink	play	bat	ring

Work with a partner, and find two meanings for each word. On a separate sheet of paper, write a sentence for each homograph.

Then, choose two pairs of homographs, and illustrate the two meanings of each word.

Share your drawings with your class.

Name _____ Date _____

Selection Vocabulary

Focus There are many different ways to practice learning new words. Scrambled words can make it fun to learn the meanings and spellings of words.

Apply

female	layer	population	balance

On a separate sheet of paper, write a sentence using each vocabulary word. If you are not sure how to use a word, find the word in "Wolf Island" to see how it was used.

On another sheet of paper, scramble the vocabulary words, and trade papers with a partner. Try to unscramble your partner's vocabulary words. Read the sentences your partner wrote. Add each word and its meaning to your vocabulary list.

Vocabulary • *Challenge Activities*

Name _____ Date _____

Making Inferences

Focus Good readers use personal experience and information from the text to gain a deeper understanding of a story. This skill is called **making inferences.**

Apply **Read the paragraph below. Work with a partner to see how many inferences you can make.**

Frankie packed his suitcase. He went downstairs and put on his coat and hat. His father kissed him goodnight. "See you tomorrow," his father called. Frankie and his grandfather walked out the door and got into the car.

What information did you use to make each inference? On a separate sheet of paper, explain each inference you made. When you finish, share your inferences and explanations with your teacher and other pairs of partners.

Name _____ Date _____

Spelling

Focus **Homographs** are words that have the same spelling, but have different pronunciations and meanings.

/ū/ can be spelled _ew and _ue.

You are a TV reporter, and you are covering the scene of a fire. You interview witnesses at the scene of the fire. On a separate sheet of paper, write your report in the form of a short script. Use dialogue from your interviews. Use at least twelve words from the list below. Try to use the challenge words *pitcher* and *nephew* in your script.

cue	few	well	rose	argue
tire	hue	ring	value	change
spew	rescue	park	view	light
	Challenge words: pitcher		nephew	

When you are finished with your script, practice reading it. Present your news report to a group of students.

Name _____ Date _____

Types of Sentences

Focus There are four types of sentences.

The four types of sentences are:

• Declarative sentences make a statement.

Example: Susan likes to paint.

• Interrogative sentences ask a question.

Example: What kind of paint do you use?

• An imperative sentence gives a command.

Example: Look at Susan's painting.

• An exclamatory sentence shows strong feeling.

Example: I love to draw!

Apply Write a skit, or a short humorous play, with a partner. Include the four types of sentences in your skit. Practice playing all the parts. Be dramatic. Use your voice to show the difference between statements, questions, demands, and exclamations. Perform your skit for another pair of partners.

Challenge Activities • Grammar, Usage, and Mechanics

Name _____ Date _____

/ī/,/ō/,/ū/, and Consonant Blends

Focus Good readers learn to identify words with **the /ī/ sound** spelled _igh, _y, and _ie. They learn to identify words with **the /ō/ sound** spelled _ow and oa_ and words with **the /ū/ sound** spelled _ue and _ew. They can also identify words that begin or end in **consonant blends.**

Apply **Read the poem below. On a separate sheet of paper, make a list of the words with the /ī/ sound spelled _igh, _y, and _ie; the /ō/ sound spelled _ow and oa_; and words with the /ū/ sound spelled _ue and _ew. Also, add words that begin or end in consonant blends.**

I know what you are thinking. You think I jumped up high
Just because you cried, "Boo!" when I was strolling by.

It wasn't you who frightened me. I just want you to know.
I only jumped because I heard the boat whistle blow.

It roared like a lion, not a teeny mew or squawk.
Now before you fall down laughing, I'll continue on my walk.

It is your turn to rhyme. On a separate sheet of paper, write two different rhymes using at least four words with the sounds and spellings that are listed above. Each rhyme should be two lines long. When you finish, read your rhymes to a partner.

Phonics • *Challenge Activities*

Name _____ Date _____

Homophones

Focus **Homophones** are words that sound the same but have different meanings and different spellings. It is important for readers to identify homophones to make sure that the right words are being used.

Apply **Read the letter below. It contains twelve homophones. Work with a partner to find them all. On a separate sheet of paper, make a list of each pair of homophones, and use each one in a sentence. Use the dictionary if you need help in finding what a word means.**

Deer Grandma and Grandpa,
We are going two the see shore next weak. Wood you like to meat us their? We can go swimming, and eye will bring a pale and shovel. After you reed this letter, right me back to tell me if ewe can come.

Love,
Tom

Name _____ Date _____

Selection Vocabulary

Focus A good way to learn vocabulary words is to use them in sentences.

Apply **All the vocabulary words below are verbs.**

appreciate	detect	exclaimed	extended	relocates	stranded

Use all the vocabulary verbs to write a realistic short story. Write your realistic story on a separate sheet of paper. Illustrate, and make a cover for your story.

When you finish, read your story to a classmate or a family member.

Vocabulary • *Challenge Activities*

Name _____ **Date** _____

Spelling

Focus **Homophones** are words that sound alike but have different spellings and different meanings.

Notice words with:

/ī/ spelled *igh*, *_y,* and *_ie.*

/ō/ spelled *_ow* and *oa.*

/ā/ spelled *a_e.*

Remember that **consonant blends** are groups of two or three letters in which the sound of each letter can be heard.

Apply **Read the poem below. Find the words that are misspelled. On a separate sheet of paper, rewrite the poem using the correct spellings.**

I went to meat him to tell him my tail.

"I need new shoes," I said with a wail.

I showed him my tow. It poked out of the seem.

My words woke him up, right out of a dream.

"Give me some piece," he said with a grown.

"I will by you a hoarse if you leave me alone."

"Do not waist your money on shoes then," I say.

"I'd rather have a hoarse than shoes any day."

Draw a cartoon to go with the poem.

Name _____ Date _____

Nouns as Subjects and Objects and Replacement Pronouns

Focus Nouns can be **subjects,** and they can also be **objects.** When a noun is an object, it receives the action from the subject. **Pronouns** such as *me, him, her, it, us,* and *them* can be used to replace a **noun object.**

Apply *Lamb Follows Mary Everywhere. Lamb Even Follows Her to School!*

Huge Spider Scares the Little Muffet Girl
Peppers Missing. Police Suspect Peter Piper

The headlines above appeared in a newspaper called the *Mother Goose Times.* On a separate sheet of paper, write six headlines with noun subjects and noun objects. You might choose to write headlines about real events or favorite books, movies, or television shows.

When you finish, trade papers with a partner. Identify the noun subjects and the noun objects. Replace the noun objects with pronouns.

Name _____ **Date** _____

/o͞o/ and /ū/ Sound/Spellings

Focus The more readers practice pronouncing words with **the /o͞o/ sound** spelled *oo, _ue, u, _ew,* and *u_e* and words with **the /ū/ sound** spelled *_ew* and *_ue,* the better they will know the words.

Apply **On a separate sheet of paper, write a story using at least one word with each of these vowel sounds:**

the /o͞o/ sound spelled *oo, _ue, u, _ew,* and *u_e*

the /ū/ sound spelled *_ew* and *_ue*

When you finish, scramble the words with the /o͞o/ and /ū/ sounds. Trade papers with a partner, and unscramble the words.

Review of Regular and Irregular Plurals, Homographs, and Homophones

Focus Students become better readers and writers when they can recognize **regular plurals, irregular plurals, homographs,** and **homophones.**

Apply **Play the Countdown Game. On a separate sheet of paper, write eight homophones, six homographs, four irregular plurals, and two regular plurals. Compare your answers with those of a partner.**

Look at the irregular plurals. Do you have any of the same answers as your partner? Discuss with your partner why some of your answers are likely to be the same.

Name _____ Date _____

Selection Vocabulary

Using vocabulary words in sentences and stories helps readers learn the words.

Use the words below to write a story about a fictional animal.

patch	habitats	rich	migrating	prey	recognize

Describe what the animal looks and sounds like. Tell how it moves and what it eats. Explain what its habitat looks like. When you use any of the vocabulary words above, underline them in your story.

Illustrate your story by drawing a picture of your animal in its habitat.

When you finish, combine your story with other students' stories, and create an animal book. Share the book with your teacher.

Name _____ Date _____

Classify and Categorize

Focus When readers **classify,** they put things or ideas into groups. When readers **categorize,** they give the groups names. **Classifying** and **categorizing** things and ideas helps readers organize their thoughts.

Apply Take four index cards. On each card, list three items that can be classified in the same category. Also list the category.

Example: List of items: feet, car, bicycle
Category: How we travel

Place the cards in front of you so that your partner cannot see the words. Use the second hand of a clock or egg timer. Read the list of items to your partner. Give your partner one minute or less to guess each category. Take turns reading your cards to each other.

When you are finished, see if you can add any items to the lists in each category.

Comprehension Skill • *Challenge Activities*

Name _____ Date _____

Spelling

Focus /o͞o/ can be spelled *oo*, *_ew*, *u_e*, *_ue*, and *u*.

Apply Last night you and your family packed a picnic and went to see a concert in the park. Today you are writing a letter to your uncle, telling him about the evening. Use at least ten words from the box below in your letter. Include the challenge words *jewel* and *duet* in your letter.

clue	tuna	root	June	flute
blue	chew	choose	glue	noodle
truth	blew	stew	duty	rude
	Challenge words:	jewel	duet	

Trade letters with a partner. Read your partner's description of the evening. How different were your letters? How did your partner use the words from the list?

Name _____   Date _____

Pronouns as Subjects

Focus   **Pronouns** can take the place of nouns. Remember that the pronoun must match the subject.

For example, if the subject is *one boy,* then the pronoun must be *he.* If the subject is *two boys,* then the pronoun must be *they.*

Apply   **Look through books with rhymes, songs, and riddles. Find seven sentences with subjects that are nouns. Make sure some of the subjects are singular and some are plural. Write each sentence on a sheet of paper.**

Trade papers with a partner, and replace the subjects with pronouns. Write the new sentence on a piece of paper. Share your sentences with another set of partners.

Name _____ Date _____

The /o͞o/ and /oo/ Sound/Spellings

Focus

Good readers practice using words with **the /o͞o/ sound** spelled *oo* and **the /oo/ sound** spelled *oo*. This helps them recognize new words in books, magazines, and newspapers.

Apply

Work with a partner, and brainstorm two lists of words. In one list, write words with the /o͞o/ sound spelled *oo*. In the other list, write words with the /oo/ sound spelled *oo*.

Working by yourself, write a story using at least three words from each list. When you finish, compare stories with your partner.

What words did you each choose? Did you choose some of the same words? Did you use the words in the same way?

Name _____ Date _____

Inflectional Ending *-ing*

**Focus** There are rules for **adding *-ing*** to base words. You have to look at the base word to know which rule you should use. The e at the end of a base word is like a stop sign. It says, "Stop, and drop me before adding *-ing*."

Apply **Play the *What am I?* game.**

My beautiful orange-and-black mother is laying her eggs under a leaf of the milkweed plant.
I am hanging from a leaf, and I look like a little green bead.
Soon I will be hatching and fluttering my new wings.

What am I?   Answer: a butterfly

Read the example above. Choose an animal, a place, a book, or even a character from a book. Work with a partner, and write at least four hints. Use at least four words with *-ing* endings. Write your hints on a separate sheet of paper, and trade papers with another pair of partners.

Word Structure • *Challenge Activities*

Selection Vocabulary

Name _____ Date _____

 Good readers practice using and spelling words to help them remember what new words mean and how to spell them.

Apply **Make up at least two rhymes using the vocabulary words in the box below.**

deal	ancient	traders	valuable
eventually	forms	kingdom	solution

Each rhyme should include at least two words from the box. The rhymes can be silly, or they can be about real things. They can even be both silly and about real things.

When you finish, share your rhymes with your family.

Name _____ Date _____

Spelling

 Focus When adding the inflectional ending *-ing*, for words with a silent *e*, drop the *e* before adding *-ing*. For words with a short vowel-consonant pattern, double the final consonant before adding *-ing*.

/**oo**/ is spelled *oo* and makes the sound as in the word *foot*.

 **Apply** **Imagine you were hiking with your family in a national park. While you are looking for wild flowers, you find something marvelous!**

On a separate sheet of paper, describe where you were hiking, what the park looked like, and what you found. Use at least ten of the words below in your description. Try to use the challenge words *woodwork* and *staring* in your writing.

took	wood	landing	brook	playing
timing	hood	batting	amazing	stood
good	hopping	hoping	shook	meaning
	Challenge words: woodwork		staring	

Draw a picture of what you found to illustrate your story. Display your story and your picture in the classroom.

Name _____ Date _____

Sentence Structure

Focus Varying the length of sentences makes writing more interesting to read.

- Combine two simple sentences to form a **compound sentence.**

- To join two sentences, use the **coordinating conjunction** *and, but, so, or, not, for,* or *yet.* Coordinating conjunctions are like glue; they hold the two sentences together.

Apply **Think of something you like to do. On a separate sheet of paper, write a paragraph about it using simple sentences. Read the simple sentences to yourself.**

Rewrite your paragraph by combining some of the sentences into compound sentences. Can you hear the difference in the way the two paragraphs sound?

When you finish, share your paragraphs with a partner.

Name _____ Date _____

The /ō/ and /ow/ Sound/Spellings

Focus

Every day, you use words with **the /ō/ sound** spelled _ow and **the /ow/ sound** spelled ow and ou_, like *know* and *town*. Finding these words is fun because there are so many of them.

Apply

Work with a partner, and brainstorm two lists. In one list, write words with the /ō/ sound spelled –ow. In the other list, write words with the /ow/ sound spelled ow and ou–. Try to add at least fifteen words to each list.

Using at least eight words from your lists, write a story about a river. The paragraph can be about the river itself, but it does not have to be. It may be about a town along the river, the weather by the river, or perhaps animals that live near or in the river.

Phonics • *Challenge Activities*

Name _____ Date _____

Inflectional Ending *-ed*

Focus When the inflectional ending *-ed* is added to the end of a base word, it lets people know that the action happened in the past.

Apply On a separate sheet of paper, write a journal entry about something that you enjoyed doing yesterday, last week, or last winter.

Trade papers with a partner. Underline each verb that ends in *-ed.* For each verb, identify the base word, and discuss with your partner how the past tense word was formed. Don't forget to date your journal.

Name _____ Date _____

Selection Vocabulary

 **Focus** Playing word games is fun! And word games help readers remember the meanings of new words.

Apply Here is an example of a backward word-chain puzzle.

Clue: 1 Down: <u>a stamp</u>

Clue: 2 Across: <u>what you owe</u>

	s		
d	e	b	t
	a		
	l		

On a separate sheet of paper, choose words from the box below, and create three backward word chains. Fill in each puzzle, and leave the clues blank. Trade papers with a partner, and figure out the clues.

counterfeit	debts	emblem	formula
inspect	portrait	remains	seal

Work with your partner to make a bigger backward word-chain puzzle with four of the words in the box. Trade puzzles with another partner group, and write the clues for the words.

Vocabulary • *Challenge Activities*

Name _____ Date _____

Sequence

Focus | **Sequence** allows readers to place events in the time order in which they occur in a story. If you know when things happen in a story, you can better understand how and why things happen.

Apply | On a separate sheet of paper, write five or six sentences that are not in the right time order. You can make up the sentences yourself, or you can look through books, magazines, or newspapers to find ideas and sentences. Trade papers with a partner, and put the sentences in the correct order.

Name _____ Date _____

Spelling

Focus
When adding the **inflectional ending -ed,** for words with a silent e, drop the e before adding -ed. For words with a short vowel-consonant pattern, double the final consonant before adding -ed. For words ending in consonant _y, change the y to i before adding -ed.

/**ow**/ is spelled ou_ and ow as in the word cow.

Apply
Write a full-page magazine advertisement that describes a hotel. Tell what is special about the hotel and why people should go there. In your ad, use at least nine words from the box below. Use the challenge words *fountain and admitted.*

browse	shower	howl	couch	stripped
striped	married	jammed	named	tried
bored	noun	loud	mouse	crowd
	Challenge words: fountain		admitted	

Illustrate your ad, and display your ad with other ads in the classroom.

Spelling • *Challenge Activities*

Name _____ **Date** _____

Adjectives

Focus **Adjectives** are words that add information to a noun or a pronoun.

Adjectives

- tell you how something looks, feels, smells, sounds, or tastes.
- tell you how many or how much.
- paint a picture in your mind as you read.

Apply **On a separate sheet of paper, write one or two paragraphs about something wonderful. It could be the discovery of something special, your favorite vacation, or it could be something great that happened to you. Use regular adjectives to describe what happened. Use comparative and superlative adjectives too. Underline all the adjectives. When you finish, read what you have written to a parent or another adult.**

Name _____ Date _____

The /aw/ Sound/Spellings

Focus Finding new words with **the /aw/ sound** spelled *aw*, *au_*, *augh*, *ough*, *all*, and *al* is a great way to become a better reader.

Apply **Read the beginning of the story below. Work with a partner, and brainstorm a list of words with the /aw/ sound spelled *aw*, *au_*, *augh*, *ough*, *all*, and *al*. On a separate sheet of paper, continue the story about Dawn's puppy. Use at least four words from your list in the story. Share your story with your teacher.**

Dawn saw the scrawny puppy. It looked awful. She caught it before it could run away, and she brought it home. "Can we keep it?" she asked.

Name _____ Date _____

Comparative and Superlative Adjectives

Focus Adjectives help you describe a picture in your mind.

- **Comparative adjectives** compare two things, people, places, or ideas.

- **Superlative adjectives** compare *more* than two things, people, places, or ideas.

Apply **Work with a partner, and write each word below on a separate index card.**

| expensive | gigantic | late | marvelous | new |
| old | pleasant | round | soft | valuable |

Turn over the cards so you cannot see the words. Take turns picking cards. When it is your turn, write one sentence using the adjective and another sentence using the superlative form of the adjective. Your partner should write one sentence using the comparative form of the adjective. Work together to help each other remember the rules for forming comparative and superlative adjectives.

Name _____ Date _____

Selection Vocabulary

Focus Using words in a new way makes them easy to remember. The more words you know, the more clearly you can describe things and ideas to other people.

Apply With a partner, create a product to sell to a new company. Your product can be something real or make-believe. Write a business letter to the new company selling your product. In your letter, describe what your product looks like, and why it is the best choice for their company. Use as many vocabulary words from the box below as you can to sell your product.

stack	profit	expenses	demand
balance	supply	product	competition

Vocabulary • *Challenge Activities*

Name _____ **Date** _____

Fact and Opinion

Focus

It is important to learn to make decisions about the information you are given. To make good decisions, you must be able to tell the difference between a **fact** and an **opinion.**

- A **fact** is something that can be proved.

- An **opinion** is what someone thinks, feels, or believes. Opinions cannot be proved.

Apply **Read the sentences below. Then, on a separate sheet of paper, write one related fact and one opinion.**

1. Whales live in the ocean.

2. A piano has keys.

3. The five senses are sight, sound, touch, taste, and feel.

4. A square has four sides.

When you finish, trade papers with a partner, and identify which sentences are fact and which are opinion.

Name _____ Date _____

Spelling

Comparative adjectives compare two or more people, things, or ideas.

Superlative adjectives compare more than two people, things, or ideas.

/aw/ is spelled *aw, au_, augh, ough, all,* and *al* and makes the sound as in the word *taught.*

Apply   You are part of a word-making group. You are in charge of the vowels *a, e, o,* and *i.* You have been given a large basket of fifteen *a*'s, one of which is a capital *A.* You have also been given a smaller basket of two *o*'s, three *e*'s, and two *i*'s. On a separate sheet of paper, complete the words by adding your vowels.

f _ ll	c _ ught	f _ st _ r	_ ugust	t _ lk
sm _ ll	f _ ught	y _ wn	b _ ught	th _ nn _ st
h _ wk	t _ ught	ch _ lk	t _ ller	_ ut _
	Challenge words: squ _ wk		h _ pp	_ _ r

Compare your answers with those of a partner. Which word or words were the hardest to complete? Why?

Spelling • *Challenge Activities*

Name _____   Date _____

Periods and Capitalization

Focus   Periods and capital letters give you important information when you read.

- A **period** tells you that a sentence has ended or that a word has been abbreviated.

- A **capital letter** tells you that a word is a special name, such as the name of a city, a river, or a building.

Apply   Pretend you are going on vacation for a week. Would you like to visit an island? A state park? Another country? You might need to look at some books and magazines to help you decide the places you would like to visit.

On a separate sheet of paper, write a list of the places you hope to see, and the days you intend to see them. Be sure to capitalize the names of locations and monuments. Use abbreviations for the days of the week and other words that are often abbreviated. When you finish, share your list with a partner.

Name _____ Date _____

The /oi/ Sound/Spellings

Focus Doing word problems with the /oi/ sound spelled *oi* and *_oy* helps readers learn to make new words.

Apply **Here are some letters and letter combinations. They can be added to make words with the /oi/ sound spelled *oi* and *_oy*.**

Word beginnings: *ann aster av b ch destr empl enj j n p sp t v*

Word endings: *age ce d l n nt se ster t*

On a separate sheet of paper, write at least ten words using one word beginning, one word ending, and the /oi/ sound spelled *oi* or *_oy*. You can use a word beginning or word ending more that once.

Then, write a paragraph using four or more of the words you made. Share your paragraph with your teacher.

Name _____ Date _____

Irregular Comparative and Superlative Adjectives

Focus There are no rules to follow to form **irregular comparative** and **superlative adjectives.** There are only a few of these adjectives, so you must practice using them to learn these adjectives.

Apply **Fill in the comparative and the superlative forms for each word.**

good	little	many	bad
_____	_____	_____	_____
_____	_____	_____	_____

Look at the words. Which words are antonyms of each other? Write your answers on a separate sheet of paper. Write a sentence using each word above. Then, write a short story using all of the sentences you have created.

Name _____ Date _____

Selection Vocabulary

Focus Thinking about new words in various ways makes them more interesting to learn.

Apply **Write your answers on a separate sheet of paper.**

1. You know what the word *millionaire* means. What do you think the word *billionaire* means?

2. Look up the words *million* and *billion* in the dictionary or in an encyclopedia. Are they real numbers? What does each one mean?

3. Look up the word *zillion* in the dictionary. Is it a real word? Is it a real number? What does the word *zillionaire* mean? How is the meaning of the word *zillionaire* different from the meanings of the words *millionaire* and *billionaire*?

Vocabulary • *Challenge Activities*

Name _____ **Date** _____

Spelling

Focus **Irregular comparative** and **superlative adjectives** are *not* formed by adding *-er* or *-est* to the ends of the words. Usually these adjectives change spellings. *worse, worst*

/oi/ is spelled *oi*, and *oy_* and makes the sound as in the word *boy*.

Apply You have just come home from seeing a show with performers and animals. Write an entry in your diary telling about what you saw. What were your favorite things? Your least favorite things? Write about your favorite animals. Use your imagination.

Use at least ten words from the box below. Notice the irregular comparative and superlative adjectives. Try to use the challenge words *employer* and *worse* in your writing.

better	royal	less	spoil	most
moist	voice	oyster	coin	best
joy	more	point	cowboy	least
	Challenge words: employer		worst	

Trade papers with a partner. Can you imagine what kind of show your partner saw from your partner's description? Which of the same words did you each use?

Challenge Activities • Spelling

Name _____   Date _____

Articles *a* and *an*

 Focus   Good writers and speakers know when to use the articles *a* and *an*.

- **The article *a*** is used before words that begin with a consonant sound.

- **The article *an*** is used before words that begin with a vowel sound.

 **Apply**   **Uh-oh! In some of the sayings below, the words *a* and *an* were left out. Other words are missing too. Work with a partner and fill in the missing articles. Then fill in the other missing words. Write your answers on a separate sheet of paper.**

1. as tall as _____ giraffe   **3.** as hot as _____ oven

2. as strong as _____ ox   **4.** as welcome as _____ skunk

Make up your own sayings. Your answer is right as long as it makes sense. If you need use another sheet of paper.

5. as _____ as _____ owl   **9.** as _____ as _____ lion

6. as _____ as _____ rock   **10.** as _____ as _____ bus

7. as _____ as _____ bear   **11.** as _____ as _____ elephant

8. as _____ as _____ eel   **12.** as _____ as _____ _____

Grammar, Usage, and Mechanics • *Challenge Activities*

Name _____ Date _____

Review of the /oi/, /aw/ /ō/, /ow/, /o͞o/ and /oo/ Sound/Spellings

Focus

The /**oi**/ sound spelled *oi* and *_oy*

The /**aw**/ sound spelled *aw*, *au_*, *augh*, *ough*, *all*, and *al*

The /**ō**/ sound spelled *_ow*

The /**ow**/ sound spelled *ow* and *ou_*

The /**o͞o**/ sound spelled *oo* and the /oo/ sound spelled *oo*

There are so many vowel sounds! The more you practice, the easier it is to recognize words with these sounds.

Apply   **Below is a sample page from a book of vowel sounds.**

The /oi/ sound spelled *oi* and *_oy*

1. coin

2. toy

Make your own book of vowel sounds. Use a separate sheet of paper for each sound found in the Focus box above.

For each sound spelling, find at least one word. Write the word, and write a sentence using the word. Draw pictures to illustrate some of the words.

When you are finished, share your book with your family.

Name _____ Date _____

Review of Inflectional Endings, and Comparative and Superlative Adjectives

Focus It is important to practice reading and writing words with the inflectional endings *-ing* and *-ed*. It is also important to practice using regular **comparative** and **superlative adjectives** and irregular comparative and superlative adjectives. Practicing makes you a better writer and reader.

Apply Write an advertisement for a product, a business, or a place. In your advertisement, use words that with inflectional endings *-ing* and *-ed*. Use regular comparative and superlative adjectives. Also use irregular comparative and superlative adjectives.

Trade advertisements with a partner, and underline the words that end in *-ing* and *-ed*. Circle the regular comparative and superlative adjectives. Put a squiggly line under the irregular comparative and superlative adjectives.

Word Structure • *Challenge Activities*

Name _____ Date _____

Selection Vocabulary

Focus While reading "Uncle Jed's Barbershop," you learned at least eight new words. Once you know the words, you will understand what they mean when you see them in another book, poem, or newspaper.

Apply The story "Uncle Jed's Barbershop" talks about barber stations at Uncle Jed's Barbershop. What other stations can you think of?

Choose a station to write about. Tell who works there. Describe what kinds of services the workers perform and what kinds of *equipment* they use.

Write your answers on a separate sheet of paper. When you finish, share your answers with a partner.

Name _____ Date _____

Spelling

Focus

/ō/ is spelled *o*, *o_e*, *_ow*, and *oa_*.

/**ow**/ is spelled *ou_* and *ow*.

/o͞o/ is spelled *oo*, *_ew*, *u_e*, *_ue*, and *u*.

/ū/ is spelled *u*, *u_e*, *_ew*, and *_ue*.

Apply You have to write about the best thing that happened last summer. You decide to write about the night that you and your friends sat around a campfire. A few people told ghost stories. On a separate sheet of paper, describe what the night was like. In your description, include at least ten words from the list below. Use the challenge words *county*, *tissue*, and *raccoon*.

glow	bonus	road	town	owl
pound	about	July	scoop	due
flew	use	rule	mule	unit

Challenge words: county   tissue   raccoon

Make a drawing to illustrate your writing.

Spelling • *Challenge Activities*

Name _____ **Date** _____

Compound Subjects and Predicates

Focus Great writers use different kinds of sentences to make reading exciting. Be a great writer.

- When a sentence has more than one subject, the subject is called a **compound subject.**

- When a sentence has more than one predicate, the predicate is called a **compound predicate.**

Apply You are a reporter for your school newspaper. Your class visited the zoo yesterday. Your job is to write an interesting news report about the visit.

On a separate sheet of paper, write your report. Be sure to use sentences with compound subjects and compound predicates. Also be sure to give your news report a headline.

When you finish, give your news report to your teacher to put up on the bulletin board.

Name _____ **Date** _____

Suffixes *-ly and -y*

 **Focus**

Adverbs describe verbs, adjectives, and other adverbs. When the **suffix *-ly*** is added to a word, the word often becomes an adverb.

Adjectives describe nouns. When the **suffix *-y*** is added to a word, the word often becomes an adjective.

Apply

Play a game called *Sometimes a Silly Sentence.* Work with a partner. Write these words on index cards, one word per card.

gentle	ice	glad	cheerful	warm
mist	noise	helpful	rain	mess
scare	sleep	immediate	slow	snow

Gather all the cards with the blank side facing up, and make a stack.

Take turns with a partner. Pick one card each. Try ending each word with *-y* and *-ly*. See what kinds of funny words you can make.

Then, add *-y* or *-ly* to each word to form an adverb or an adjective correctly. Write a sentence using the adjective or adverb you just created. Sometimes you might have to make the sentence a bit silly. Have fun! Keep picking cards until you have changed all the words into adverbs or adjectives.

Word Structure • *Challenge Activities*

Name _____ Date _____

Suffixes *-ment* and *-tion*

Focus | The **suffixes *-ment*** and ***-tion*** mean "action" or "process." When the suffix *-ment* or *-tion* appears at the end of a word, it is usually a clue that the word is a noun.

Apply | On a separate sheet of paper make a list of the words below, and add *-ment* or *-tion* to each word to make a noun.

enjoy	celebrate	entertain	detect	move
govern	invent	act	involve	attract

Then, write a newspaper story using at least four of the words. Illustrate your story. What interesting news story can you tell with the words you created?

When you are finished, combine your story with other students' stories to make a group newspaper.

Name _____ Date _____

Selection Vocabulary

Focus The vocabulary words you are learning from the story "Sun" are words scientists use every day.

Apply Congratulations! You have just discovered a new planet in our solar system. Write a letter to the journal *New Space Discoveries* to describe your planet. The address is 6 Million Outerspace Drive, Washington, D.C. 00000. Send your letter to the Editor of New Discoveries.

In your letter, use at least five of the words below.

bursts	devices	slightly	oval
tilted	horizon	solar system	orbit

In the body of your letter, try to answer these questions:

- How did you discover your planet? Did you design something special for looking into space so you could see it?

- What does the new planet look like? What color or colors is it?

- What is it probably made of?

- What planets are close by?

- What would you like to name it? Why?

Be sure to include the name of the journal, the address, and a greeting. When you finish, look at the vocabulary words again. Which words do you think scientists use? Why?

Vocabulary • *Challenge Activities*

Name _____ Date _____

Drawing Conclusions

Focus People use information from what they read or see to **draw conclusions** about a character, an event, or about information that is not stated directly. Conclusions must be supported by details.

Apply **Think about a movie you have seen lately or about a book you have read. How did you tell the difference between the good and the bad characters?**

Choose a movie, television show, or book. Pick a character. How do you know if the character is good or bad? How did you draw your conclusion? On a separate sheet of paper, write at least three reasons for your conclusion.

Include

• the name of the movie, book, or television show.

• what the movie, book, or television show is about.

• the character's name.

• what the character did or said to make you reach your conclusion.

When you finish, share your writing with a partner.

Name _____ **Date** _____

Spelling

> **Focus**
>
> The suffix **-ly** can be added to some words. Adding -ly can make some words an adverb. An adverb tells about a verb, an adjective, or another adverb.
>
> The suffix **-y** can be added to some nouns. Adding -y can make a word an adjective. An adjective tells about a noun.
>
> The suffixes **-ment** and **-tion** mean "action" or "process."

Most of the words in the box below are mixed up. On a separate piece of paper, rewrite each word with its correct suffix. Keep in mind that two words are correct as they are.

actly	inventy	selectment	statement	treation
chewtion	payly	apartly	scarly	slighty
easiment	kindy	partion	shiply	daiment
rusty	bonment			

Spelling • *Challenge Activities*

Name _____ Date _____

Commas

Focus

When a writer lists things, the list is called a **series.** When the series has three or more items, commas are added between each item.

A comma also follows the words *yes* and *no* at the beginning of a sentence.

Apply **Read the poem below, then add the missing commas.**

Take an apple a peach and a pear
And slice them up quite neat.
Put them on a plate
And please have some to eat.

Do you like them?
Are they delicious?

Yes I find them
Quite nutritious.

Take a cracker some cheese
And an olive.

Pour some juice into a cup.
Put everything on your tray
And please eat it all up.

Do you like them?
Do you find them delightful?

No I'm too full.
Not one more biteful!

Write a list of six to nine items, such as food items, types of things found outdoors, or items of clothing. Write a poem of your own using these lists. Use commas in series and commas after the words *yes* and *no* at the beginning of a line. Share your poetry with the class.

Name _____ Date _____

Suffixes *-ful* and *-able*

Focus The suffix **-ful** means "to be full of." The suffix **-able** means "inclined to be" something. What happens when you add the suffix *-able* to a word that ends in *e*? You drop the e, and then you add *-able.*

Apply **Pretend you and your partner are taking a walk. On your walk, you discover a marvelous device.**

In two or three paragraphs, describe it:

• What does it look like?

• What does it do?

• Can you change it to make it even better?

• Does it make noise?

In your description, make sure you use at least four words that end in *-ful* and four words that end in *-able.* Look at the lists below. They will help you get started.

wonderful	**frightful**	**fixable**	**wearable**
successful	**joyful**	**drivable**	**likable**
colorful	**dutiful**	**movable**	**mistakable**
delightful	**truthful**	**washable**	**acceptable**

When you finish, share your writing with your teacher.

Word Structure • *Challenge Activities*

Name _____ Date _____

Inflectional Endings *-ed* and *-ing*

Focus Adding the **endings -ed** and **-ing** to a base verb changes the tense of the verb.

Adding *-ed* makes the verb past tense. Adding *-ing* shows present or continuous action.

When the base verb has a consonant-vowel-consonant pattern, double the final consonant before you add *-ed* or *-ing*.

Apply Fred and Bing were studying verbs. Fred looked up from his book and said, "Look, do you see the verb *play?* I can change that to *played!* Do you see that, Bing? Do you see the *-ed?* That's the same as the end of my name!"

"Well," Bing answered, "I can do that too, you know. With the last letters of my name, I can form the word *playing.* All I have to do is add *-ing.* Ha!"

"I bet I can get more words than you can," Fred challenged.

If you were Bing, how would you respond to Fred? On a separate sheet of paper, write your answer. Then, list five more verbs that both Fred and Bing could change. Write the changes for them.

When you finish, think about different verbs. Do you think Fred is right? Do you think he can find more verbs that end in *-ed* than end in *-ing?* Explain your answer.

Name _____ Date _____

Selection Vocabulary

Focus Good writers choose words that create pictures in your mind. The word *bald* is a good example. What do you see in your mind when you hear that word? Some words, such as *crackle,* can even make you hear sounds in your mind.

Apply **What do you see in your mind when you read the following words? Write your answers on a separate sheet of paper.**

directions   sneak   bushy   squinty   ringed   clay   tight   rays

Make a picture book using each of the vocabulary words in the list above. Write two or three sentences describing the picture that each word brings to mind. Use a separate page for each word. Illustrate each page.

When you finish, share your book with a parent or another adult.

Name _____ Date _____

Author's Purpose

Focus Identifying the **author's purpose** helps readers understand the ideas in a text. If you are reading a funny advertisement, it may be entertaining, but you know that the author's purpose is to persuade you to buy something. Paying attention to details is a good way to identify the author's purpose.

Apply **Work with a partner. Review the three main purposes for writing:**

- To inform

- To entertain

- To persuade

Choose two purposes. Together decide what you would like to write about. You can look through books and magazines to get ideas.

Write one paragraph for each purpose. The paragraphs do not have to be about the same idea. Reread what you wrote. Did you add details that show the purpose?

When you finish, each of you read one paragraph to another team of partners. See if the partners can guess the purpose of each paragraph.

Name _____ Date _____

Spelling

Focus
The suffix **-ful** means "full of." The suffix **-able** means "able" or "tending to be."

Remember, the **inflectional ending -ed** shows an action that happened in the past.

The **inflectional ending -ing** shows an action that is happening now.

Apply
Suppose you were given your own small flying machine to use for an hour. In a paragraph or two, write what you might do. Use at least ten words from below. Try to use the challenge words *wonderful* and *injured* in your writing.

ringed	painful	fixable	scared	helpful
filling	pleasing	wishful	notable	stunning
wearable	dressing	clogged	harmful	likable
	Challenge words: wonderful		injured	

When you are done, read your paragraph to your teacher.

Spelling • *Challenge Activities*

Name _____ **Date** _____

Compound Words and Contractions

Focus Both **compound words** and **contractions** are formed by joining two different words. When making contractions, some letters are taken out, and an apostrophe is added to show where the letters are missing.

If you know how to form compound words and contractions, then you can also figure out how to take them apart.

Apply

1. Solve these word-addition problems.

any	some	every	no
+ one	+ body	+ where	+ thing
_____	_____	_____	_____

2. Solve these word-subtraction problems.

anybody	somewhere	everyone	nobody
– any	–	–	– body
	where	every	

3. Solve these word problems by changing the words into contractions.

I am = _____   you are = _____   have not = _____

4. Solve these word problems by changing the contractions into two words.

isn't = _____   couldn't = _____   you'll = _____

Name _____ Date _____

Suffixes -ity and -less

Focus

The **suffix -ity** means "state of being." For words that end in e, drop the e, and then add -ity.

The **suffix -less** means "without" or "lacking." Just attach it to the end of the base word.

Apply Start a suffix book. Write the suffix -ity across the top of a sheet of paper. On the left side of the paper, list at least ten words to which you can add the suffix -ity. Here are some words to start with. On the right side, write each word with the suffix added.

active   equal   humid

Make another set of pages for your book, but this time use the suffix -less. Start with the words below.

fear   sound   taste

When you finish, look at the words you made with the suffix -less.

Now, choose three of the words you made for -ity and three for -less. Use each word in a sentence. Write the sentences on a new sheet of paper. Put the papers together so they face each other like a book. Save your book so you can add pages to it later.

Word Structure • *Challenge Activities*

Name _____ Date _____

Suffixes *-ness* and *-sion*

Focus

The suffixes **-ness** and **-sion** mean "state of being."

To add the suffix *-ness* to most words, just attach it at the end.

- For words that end in *-y*, first change the *y* to an *i*. Then, add *-ness.*

To add the suffix *-sion:*

- For words that end in *ss*, drop one *s* and then add *-sion* to the end of the word.

- For most words that end in *e*, drop the *e*, and add *-sion.*

- For words that end in *de* or *se*, take away the *de* or *se*. Then, add *-sion.*

Apply

Continue adding to your suffix book. Use the suffixes *-ness* and *-sion*. List ten words to add to each suffix. Write each word with the suffix added. Then, choose three words, and use each of them in a sentence. Write the sentences on a second sheet of paper, and add them to your book.

Here are some words to start with.

good	dark	friendly
decide	confuse	impress

When you finish, make a cover for your book.

Name _____ Date _____

Selection Vocabulary

Focus

Suppose you say that the moon looks like a lemon slice. You might be thinking of half a slice of lemon, but the person you are describing the moon to might be thinking of a whole, round slice.

However, if you say the moon is a first quarter moon, people will know exactly what you mean. When you know the right scientific words, you can describe ideas and objects clearly.

Apply **Work with a partner. Below are the phases of the moon.**

new moon waxing crescent moon first quarter	full moon last quarter waning crescent moon

On a big piece of poster paper, make a moon chart. Write the phases along the bottom. Then, draw an illustration of the moon in each phase. Use books or the Internet to see what the phases look like.

Do research to find out when the next new moon and full moon will occur. Write the dates next to the correct phases. Share the dates with your family so you can look at the sky together on those nights.

Vocabulary • *Challenge Activities*

Name _____ **Date** _____

Compare and Contrast

Focus

You can **compare** and **contrast** what you see in pictures and what you read in books. In books, look for phrases such as *the same as, smaller than,* and *bigger than.*

- **Comparing** means telling how things, events, or characters are alike.

- **Contrasting** means telling how things, events, or characters are different.

Apply

Pick two of your favorite books, pictures, songs, or poems. On a separate sheet of paper, for each favorite that you chose, write the title, the author's or artist's name, and describe each one.

Then, contrast and compare your two favorites. Tell at least three ways in which they are alike and three ways in which they are different. When you finish, share your writing with your teacher.

Name _____ Date _____

Spelling

Focus

The suffixes **-ity** and **-ness** mean "state of being."

The suffix **-less** means "without."

The suffix **-tion** means "the action of something." Sometimes the suffix -tion is spelled -sion.

Apply

Choose at least eight of the words below, and illustrate each word. You can add as many as two illustrations on a page. Under each drawing, write the word in cursive. Use the challenge words *breathless* and *explosion* as two of your eight illustrations.

weakness	tension	sleepless	rarity	endless
sanity	fitness	priceless	purity	erosion
blindness	electricity	fairness	division	careless
	Challenge words: breathless		explosion	

Choose one drawing, and hide the word with your hand or a piece of paper. Ask a partner to guess the word from your illustration.

Name _____ Date _____

Adverbs and Combining Sentences

Adverbs are words that describe a verb, an adjective, or another adverb. Adverbs tell *how, when, where,* or *how much* something happens.

Many adverbs end with the suffix *-ly.* However, some words that end in *-ly* are not adverbs, so be careful!

Varying the lengths of sentences makes writing more interesting. One way to vary the length of a sentence is to combine two short sentences into one.

Apply In a magazine or newspaper article, find five short, simple sentences that include an adverb. Copy the sentences onto a separate sheet of paper. Underline the adverb in each sentence.

Read the sentences again. Write a new short sentence that can be combined with the sentence you found. Combine the sentences together. Do this for all five sentences.

Choose one of the five combined sentences. Make a drawing that illustrates the sentence. Use the sentence for a caption by writing it below your drawing.

When you finish, put your cartoon into a book with cartoons drawn by other students. Take turns reading the book of cartoons and identifying the adverbs in the captions.

Name _____ Date _____

Greek Root Words: *ast, graph, log,* and *scop*

Focus Many words in English have ancient Greek roots. Think of people thousands of years ago using the same roots we use today!

- *ast* and *astr* mean "star."
- *graph* means "write" or "draw."
- *log* and *logue* mean "word" or "speak."
- *scop* means "see" or "observe."

Apply Make a Greek roots dictionary. Choose one word from each group below, or choose your own word. Look up the word in the dictionary to find out what the word means. What does the dictionary tell you about the different parts of the word?

- asteroid, aster, asterisk, astronomer

- autograph, graphologist, paragraph, photograph

- epilogue, logogram, monologue

- endoscope, kaleidoscope, microscope, periscope, telescope

Write the definition of the word on a separate sheet of paper. Then, give an example of the word in a sentence, and draw or find a picture you can place below your sentence.

Save your dictionary so you can add more vocabulary words.

Word Structure • *Challenge Activities*

Name _____   Date _____

Latin Root Words: *grat, mar, miss,* and *port*

Focus

Thousands of years ago, the people who lived in Rome spoke Latin. Many words in English have Latin roots. Knowing what a root means can help you figure out the meaning of a new word with that root.

Here are some Latin roots:

- *grat* is "pleasing."
- *mar* is "sea."

- *miss* is "send."
- *port* is "carry."

Apply

Make a Latin roots dictionary. Choose one word from each group below, or choose your own word. Look up the word in the dictionary to find out what the word means. What does the dictionary tell you about the different parts of the word?

- congratulations, grateful, ungrateful

- aquamarine, mariner, submarine

- missile, mission, missive

- portfolio, reporter, transportation

Use a separate sheet of paper for each word. Write the definition of the word. Then, give an example of the word in a sentence, draw a picture of it, or find a picture you can paste below your sentence. When you finish, share your dictionary with your teacher. Save your dictionary so you can add vocabulary words.

Name _____ Date _____

Selection Vocabulary

Focus Root words help you understand and remember new words.

Apply **Answer each of the following questions on a separate sheet of paper.**

1. **Study the word *astronaut*.** You already know what *astr* means. What does *naut* mean? What root is *naut* related to? You can find out by looking up the word *nautical* in the dictionary. Is the root Latin or Greek?

    Write the definition of *astronaut*. Then, give an example of the word, draw a picture of it, or find a picture you can paste below your definition.

2. **Find the word *gigantic* in the dictionary.** What is its root? Is it Latin or Greek? Write the definition of *gigantic*. Then, give an example of the word, draw a picture of it, or find a picture you can paste below your definition.

3. **Find the word *orbit* in the dictionary.** What is its root? Is it Latin or Greek? Write the definition of *orbit*. Then give an example of the word, draw a picture of it, or find a picture you can paste below your definition.

When you finish, add each answer to your Greek or Latin roots book.

Vocabulary • *Challenge Activities*

Name _____ **Date** _____

Spelling

Focus **Latin roots** are word parts that come from Latin.

The root **grat** means "thankful or pleasing"; **mar** means "sea or ocean"; **miss** means "sent"; and **port** means "carry."

Greek roots are word parts that come from Greek.

The root **ast** means "star"; **graph** means "something written or drawn"; **log** (sometimes spelled *logue*) means "to speak"; **scop** means "to look at or examine."

Apply The first woman to land on the moon has come to your school to speak. The students are allowed to ask questions after she finishes her speech. Write two paragraphs that tell about what she said. Then create a list of questions that you might like to ask.

Use at least ten words from the box below in your writing. Include the challenge words *biography* and *microscope* in your writing.

grateful	mission	report	autograph	astronaut
dialogue	import	marine	photograph	mariner
dismiss	gratitude	astronomy	apology	telescope
	Challenge words: biography		microscope	

Name _____ Date _____

Synonyms and Antonyms

Focus

A **synonym** is a word that has the same or almost the same meaning as another word. Synonyms make writing more exciting.

An **antonym** is a word that means the opposite or nearly the opposite of another word. Antonyms show the difference between two things.

Apply Work with a partner. Write each word on an index card.

bald	difficult	freezing
near	noise	rapid
scream	small	terrible
toss	under	find

Put the cards word-side down. Take turns choosing cards. The person who chooses the card can decide whether to give an antonym or a synonym for the word. The partner must give the other.

Keep a list of each word with its synonym and antonym. Try to add more synonyms and antonyms to your lists.

Grammar, Usage, and Mechanics • *Challenge Activities*

Name _____ **Date** _____

Review of *-ly, -y, -ment, -tion, -ful, -able, -ed,* and *-ing*

Focus In this unit, you learned about different word endings. You studied the **suffixes**

- *-ly*
- *-y*
- *-ment*

- *-able*
- *-ful*
- *-tion*

and the **inflectional endings** *-ed* and *-ing.*

Apply You and your friend are lying on the grass, looking at the clouds in the sky. "Look," you say to your friend, "do you see what that cloud looks like? Oh, and the one next to it? Look at what it resembles!"

In one or two paragraphs, describe what your imaginary sky looks like and what the clouds resemble. In your descriptions, use words that end with the suffixes *-ly, -y, -ment, -tion, -ful,* and *-able.* Make sure you use each suffix at least once. Also use at least one word each with the inflectional endings *-ed* and *-ing.*

When you have finish writing, look through your paragraphs to find the words with the different word endings. List the words on a separate sheet of paper, and explain what each one means.

Name _____ Date _____

Review of *-ity, -less, -ness, -sion,* and Greek and Latin Root Words

Focus Good readers are also good word detectives. They know how to find clues in words—such as suffixes and roots—to help them understand the words they are reading. The suffixes and roots you learned in this unit will help you become a good word detective.

Apply **Work with a partner. Each of you should write an example of a word with the following word parts:**

- *-ity*

- *-less*

- *-ness*

- *-sion*

- *ast* or *astr*

- *graph*

- *log* or *logue*

- *scop*

- *grat*

- *mar*

- *miss*

- *port*

Tell whether the part is a suffix or a root. If it is a suffix, explain what the suffix means. If it is a root, explain what the root means. Then, tell whether the root is Greek or Latin.

Name _____ Date _____

Selection Vocabulary

 Focus Acting out new words can make them easier to remember. The more words you remember, the more clearly you can describe things and ideas to other people.

 **Apply** **Try to describe things and ideas *without* words. *Pantomlme* is a kind of acting where the actor does not speak any words. Instead, the actor just uses actions.**

Work with a partner, and decide how you would pantomime each of the words below. Reread the story "Earth" to check the meaning of the words before you begin.

astronomers   top   curve   rotation   scraped

Now try these words. You may find them harder to pantomime than the words above. If you cannot think of a way to pantomime the meaning, how else might you show what the words mean without talking?

atmosphere   scale   signs

When you finish, choose three vocabulary words to pantomime. Then, pantomime them for another team of partners. Discuss with the other team how you could show the meaning of the words that were the most difficult to pantomime.

Name _____ Date _____

Spelling

Focus The suffixes *-ly, -y, -ment, -ful, -able, -ity, -less, -ness,* and *-sion* can be added to the end of a word to change the meaning of the word.

When the **inflectional ending *-ing*** is added to a base verb, it shows that the action is happening now. The **inflectional ending *-ed*** shows that the action happened in the past.

Some words have **roots** that come from **Latin** and **Greek**.

Apply You are standing at the top of the Grand Canyon. On a separate sheet of paper, write a letter to your grandmother. Tell her about what you see and how different it is from the large city in which she lives. Include at least ten of the words below. Use the challenge words *advertisement* and *amusing* in your letter.

scary	kindly	pleasing	clogged	harmful
erosion	careless	statement	mariner	grateful
import	notable	electricity	weakness	telescope

Challenge words: advertisement   amusing

Make a drawing to accompany your letter.

Spelling • *Challenge Activities*

Name _____ Date _____

Subject and Verb Agreement

Focus The **subject** of a sentence **must agree with the verb.** Both must be either singular or plural. When the subject and the verb *do not* agree, the meaning of the sentence is not clear.

Apply Look at each underlined word. Change the word *only* if it is wrong, to make the subject and the verb agree. Cross out each wrong answer, and write the correct answer close to the crossed-out word.

Rain
by Robert Louis Stevenson

The rain <u>are</u> raining all around.
It <u>fall</u> on field and tree.
<u>They</u> rains on the umbrellas here
And on the ships at sea.

The Lazy Roof
By Gelett Burgess

The roof it <u>have</u> a lazy time
A-lying in the sun;
The walls, they <u>has</u> to hold him up;
They do not <u>have</u> much fun!

A Walk in the Woods
Sarah and Sue <u>are</u> singing a song
As they <u>goes</u> happily hiking along.
"Uh-oh," Sarah <u>say</u>. "What <u>are</u> that I <u>sees</u>?"
As a little brown bear <u>runs</u> up a tree.
Sarah and Sue <u>continues</u> their walk.

When you finish, read the corrected poems, and listen to them in your mind as you read. Listen to how much easier it is to understand them when the subject and verb agree.

Name _____ Date _____

Prefixes *re-* and *un-*

Focus

When you know what a prefix means, it can help you figure out the meaning of a word. The prefix *re-* often means "again." The prefix *un-* often means "not."

Apply

Work with a partner to write a sentence for each pair of words below. On a separate sheet of paper, use both words in a sentence. The words do not have to be in the same order as they are shown.

1. refreeze   reheat   **6.** unusual   unknown

2. rewrite   unfair   **7.** rebroke   refixed

3. refold   uneven   **8.** unsure   replant

4. unalike   unequal   **9.** reopen   unafraid

5. repaint   reclean   **10.** unwise   reuse

Choose a sentence to read to your class.

Name _____ Date _____

Prefixes *pre-* and *mis-*

Focus The prefix *pre-* often means "before" or "beforehand."
The prefix *mis-* often means "wrong" or "bad."

Apply

| predawn | preschool | presweetened | pregame | predate |
| mislay | miswrite | misdate | misinform | misjudge |

Choose a word from the box above for each sentence below. Write the word that fits best on the line.

1. I like cereal without sugar. Most brands at the store are too sweet

because they are sugared before they are packaged. _____

2. I can't find my book anywhere! I know I put it down somewhere last

night. _____

3. What is one of the quietest times of day? I think it is the time just

before the sun starts to rise. _____

4. Something seems wrong. This letter says it was written on September

18, 3000. _____

Look at sentence 4. Can you find another word from the list that would make a good answer? On a separate sheet of paper, write sentences for the remaining words in the box.

Name _____ Date _____

Selection Vocabulary

Focus The more often you use new words, the better you will know them.

Apply **Imagine you have a treasure. You cannot take it with you, so you have to hide it. You need to make a treasure map so you can find it again.**

Work with a partner. Make a treasure map, and write a story about the treasure and where you have hidden it. Use at least six of the selection vocabulary words in your story.

fierce   burrows   sturdy   trickle
stump   crumbling   settlers   treasures

As you write your story, think about the answers to these questions:

In what year are you living? In what place are you living?

What is your treasure? Where did you get your treasure?

Why are you not able to take your treasure with you?

How will you choose a place to hide it?

When you finish, display your map and story in the classroom.

Name _____ Date _____

Author's Purpose

Focus

Once readers understand an **author's purpose** for writing, they can better understand the text and know what to expect. You can discover the author's purpose by paying attention to details in a text.

Apply

Find a magazine in your classroom or school library. Choose an article you think is interesting. Answer the questions on a separate sheet of paper.

What is the title of the article? What is the author's name? What is the article about?

Do the details in the article make you laugh or feel sad or happy? Explain your answer, and give three or more reasons.

Do the details in the article make you want to keep reading? Explain your answer, and give three or more details.

Does the article give you information about a place or a person or an event? Explain your answer.

Why do you think the author wrote the article? Do you think he or she has more than one purpose? Why?

Are there illustrations? Do they help show the author's purpose? How?

When you finish, share your answers with a partner.

Name _____ Date _____

Spelling

Focus   A word changes meaning when a prefix is added to the beginning of the word.

The prefix:

re- means "again."

un- means "not" or "opposite of."

pre- means "before."

mis- means "wrong" or "bad."

Apply   **Ollie added the prefixes *re-, un-, pre-,* and *mis-* to the group of words he was given. He attached the prefixes to the right words, but sometimes he added them at the beginning of the words and sometimes at the end. Also, he often mixed up the order of the letters in the prefixes. On a separate sheet of paper, respell the words so they each begin with the prefix. Make sure the letters of the prefix are in the right order.**

matchism	nuclear	reader	erfund	zipun	printsim
loadun	leadsmi	perheat	starter	fixerp	fairun
countre	placesim	viewpre	repschool	awarenu	

Work with a partner to decode Ollie's note of apology. This is what he said.

"I am sorry about the matchism! I was awarenu that
I mixed up each fixerp."

Spelling • *Challenge Activities*

Name _____ Date _____

Verb Tenses

Focus

The **tense** of a verb tells you *when* an action happens.

- **Present tense** verbs tell what is happening now or what happens all the time.

- **Past tense** verbs, often formed by adding *-ed* to the base word, tell what has already happened. Some verbs are irregular, and their forms must be learned.

- **Future tense** verbs tell what will happen in the future. The helping verb *will* is used for the future tense.

Apply

You are part of a television news team. Your job is to report on the weather. Every night at 6:15 you give your weather report. Today, the weather in your area is changing very quickly.

Write a weather report that describes what the weather was like earlier that day. Then, tell what the weather is usually like for that time of year. Finally, explain what you think the weather will be like the next day. Underline the present, past, and future tenses in your report.

Make a big weather map to go with your report.

When you finish, present your weather report to a partner. Refer to your weather map as you give your report.

After you and your partner have given your reports, discuss these questions together:

Where did you use the present tense? Where did you use the past tense? For which part did you use the future tense?

Name _____ Date _____

The Prefix *bi-* and *mid-*

Focus

The prefix **bi-** means "two."

The prefix **mid-** means "being the part in the middle." It begins many compound words.

Apply Use the prefix *bi-* to make a small book. Use index cards for the pages. On each page, write one word that begins with the prefix *bi-.* Write the definition of the word, and then draw an example of it. Here is a list of bases you can choose from. You can also add your own words to the list. Your book should be at least four pages long. Use a dictionary to help you.

color	cycle	monthly	plane
cuspid	lingual	ped	valve

Now make a small *mid-* book. Make the *mid-* book the same way that you made the *bi-* book. Add your own words. Use a dictionary to help you.

day	night	point
stream	summer	winter

When you finish, make a cover for each of your books. Share your books with your family.

Word Structure • *Challenge Activities*

Name _____ Date _____

Prefixes *dis-* and *auto-*

Focus The prefix *dis-* means "opposite of." The prefix *auto-* means "self."

Apply You are a reporter for your school newspaper. A famous author is coming to your school. This author just published an autobiography. After speaking to the school, the author will take questions from the press.

On a separate sheet of paper, write a few interview questions that you would like to ask the author, and create the imagined author's answers. Use at least three words with the prefix *dis-* and three words with the prefix *auto-*. You can choose from the list below if you wish.

disapprove	disconnect	disobey	autograph
disbelieve	discover	autobiography	automatic

Write up your interview for the school paper. Be sure to include the author's name and the book title in your report.

Name _____ Date _____

Selection Vocabulary

**Focus** The more you use vocabulary words, the better you will know them the next time you come across them in your reading.

Apply **Each sentence below is the beginning of a different story. Choose two, and write stories that begin with the sentences. Your stories should be at least three paragraphs long. Use a different sheet of paper for each story. Give each story a title and an illustration.**

The rain **beats** down, soaking everything it touches.

Today I **charted** an island where no one has been before.

I walked into the **laboratory,** ready to go to work.

I felt a **challenge** to design an even better car than the one I designed before.

My family has special **customs.**

As I looked around, I thought to myself, "What in the world could cause this **ruin?**"

When you finish, read your stories to your family.

Name _____ Date _____

Spelling

Focus **Place words** are words that reveal the location of objects.

A word changes meaning when a prefix is added.

The prefix

bi- means "every two" or "twice."

mid- means "in the middle of."

dis- means "not."

auto- means "self."

Apply Imagine you are a famous author who is going to talk on TV about your newest book. You are late in arriving at the TV show. Use at least ten words in the box to write two paragraphs explaining why you were late, how you got there, and what your book is about. Use the challenge words *disagree* and *autobiography* in your writing.

disprove	bifocal	autograph	upon	midsummer
distrust	biplane	automatic	midtown	within
automobile	near	midweek	disband	bicycle

Challenge words: disagree   autobiography

Trade papers with a partner. Look for the challenge words. How did your partner use them?

Name _____ Date _____

Prepositions and Prepositional Phrases

Focus Prepositions and prepositional phrases are common to the English language.

Prepositions show position or direction of a noun or pronoun.

Example: *up, down, in, on, over, from, under, to, above, below, across, by*

Prepositional phrases begin with a preposition and end with a noun or pronoun. They add details that help describe an idea, a thing, a person, or an event.

Example: *up the tree, in the car, across the street, by the road*

Apply **Work with a partner. Make a list of eight prepositions. Choose four prepositions each, and write a prepositional phrase with each preposition. Use each prepositional phrase in a sentence, and then draw a cartoon picture to go with the sentence. Write the sentence below your drawing so it becomes a caption for the cartoon. A cartoon is a simple drawing. It does not have to be funny. When you finish, create an art exhibit that shows the cartoons you and your partner made.**

Grammar, Usage, and Mechanics • *Challenge Activities*

Name _____   Date _____

Affixes as Syllables

Focus   An **affix** is a group of letters that is added to a base word. **Prefixes** and **suffixes** are types of affixes. Sometimes an affix can add more than one syllable to a base word.

The suffix **-able** is two syllables.

> Example: read (one syllable) → read*able* (three syllables)

The prefix **auto-** is two syllables

> Example: pilot (two syllables) → *auto*pilot (four syllables)

Apply   **Read the conversation below. Underline the words that have affixes. Copy those words on a separate sheet of paper. Divide each word into syllables. Circle the prefixes. Place a box around a blue marker or pen to underline the suffixes. When you say the words to yourself, can you hear that the prefixes and suffixes are their own syllables?**

"Suppose you had a handful of coins and you dropped one as you went to the store. What would you do?" Frankie asked.

"I would retrace my steps to find it," answered Grandmother promptly.

"But suppose it was a windy, freezing day. Would you take the same action?" he asked.

"Hmmm," Grandmother said. "I would rethink my plan and look carefully on the way back."

Name _____ Date _____

Affixes Used to Change Word Meanings

Focus When good readers study words with affixes, they can detect how the **affixes change the meaning** of the base words. Sometimes an affix can even make the base word mean its opposite.

Apply Identify the prefixes and suffixes in each of the following words. On a separate sheet of paper, explain the meaning of each affix. Which affixes make a word mean its opposite?

beautiful	misplace
bimonthly	readable
careless	refill
doable	retie
endless	thankful
hairless	unopened
hopeful	unplanned

Choose at least four of the words. Write a journal entry about a special day using those words. When you finish, share your journal entry with your family.

Word Structure • *Challenge Activities*

Name _____ Date _____

Selection Vocabulary

 **Focus** Learning synonyms and antonyms for new vocabulary words is a great way to remember their meanings.

 **Apply** **Work with a partner. Each of you choose three words from the box below.**

clerk	rumble	shattered	exactly
damaged	tough	frames	section

Write each word you chose on an index card. On the back of the card, write one synonym and one antonym for each word. Place the synonym and antonym side of the card down. Have your partner read the first vocabulary word aloud, and try to guess the synonym and the antonym of the word that your partner chose. After you both have traded turns, work together to find more synonyms and antonyms for each vocabulary word.

Name _____ Date _____

Fact and Opinion

 **Focus** It is important to make decisions about the information you read. You must be able to tell the difference between a fact and an opinion.

A **fact** is something true that can be proven.

An **opinion** is what someone thinks, feels, or believes. An opinion cannot be proven.

Apply **Read the letter below. On a separate sheet of paper, list at least four facts and four opinions from the letter.**

Dear Uncle Theo,

Today is my birthday. I am eight years old. We went to the toy store, and I used the birthday money you sent me. I bought the best toy! It is a car that changes into a plane that then changes into a monster. It has flashing red and blue lights, and it makes rumbling and screeching sounds. It is so cool! Even the clerk in the toy store said it was the greatest!

Thank you for the birthday money.

Your nephew, Vincent

When you finish, share your answers with a partner. Did you both choose the same facts and same opinions?

Comprehension Skill • *Challenge Activities*

Spelling

Focus | **Affixes** are suffixes and prefixes that are added to base words. They are their own syllables in words. Affixes are used to change the meanings of words.

Apply | **Here is the beginning of a story.**

Luke and Erica were sitting at the top of the hill when the bells in the tower rang twelve times.

Finish the story using at least ten words from the box below. Try to include the challenge words *exactly* and *disconnect* in your story.

lucky	unlucky	freeze	antifreeze	rest
restful	restless	fade	miswrite	count
discount	move	movement	tell	retell

Challenge words: exactly disconnect

Illustrate your story. When you have finished, display your story in the classroom.

Sentence Tense

Focus

Good readers know that **verb tenses** tell you whether a sentence happened in the **past,** is happening in the **present,** or will happen in the **future.**

Remember that you can form the past tense of many verbs by adding *-ed* at the end of the base verb. You can often form the future tense of a verb by adding the helping verb *will.*

Apply

You are taking a vacation in a beautiful place. You arrived yesterday. Write a letter to your friend describing what you see. Write your letter on a separate sheet of paper. Leave a little room between your sentences so you can add something later.

In your letter

• tell your friend what you did yesterday.

• describe what you are seeing as you write your letter.

• explain what you are going to do tomorrow.

When you finish, identify whether a sentence is in the past, present, or future tense by writing the word "past," "present," or "future" in the space you left next to each sentence. Remember to add a greeting and a closing to your letter.

Name _____ Date _____

Word Families

Copyright © SRA/McGraw-Hill. Permission is granted to reproduce this page for classroom use.

Focus

A group of words that are all formed from the same base word make up a **word family.** When you know how words are connected, you can better understand the meaning of the words.

Apply

Work with a partner. On a separate sheet of paper, add words to create word families for each base word below.

act	animate	breathe	build	freeze	frighten
joy	live	move	snow	try	write

Next, choose four word families, and draw an illustration that best represents each family. Use a different sheet of paper for each word family you choose. Write the words around your illustrations. Your illustrations should give a general idea of each word family's meaning.

When you've finished, share your papers with your teacher.

Name _____ Date _____

Multisyllabic Words with Silent Consonants

Focus

Some words with many syllables have a silent consonant. A **silent consonant** does not add a sound to a word.

- **ck** makes a /k/ sound. The c is silent.
- **sc** makes an /s/ sound when it is followed by the vowel e or i.
- **kn** makes an /n/ sound. The k is silent.
- Together the vowel **i** and the consonants **gh** make a /ī/ sound.

Apply

Each of the words below has at least one silent consonant. How many syllables does each word have? Divide the words below into syllables. Answer the question at the end of each group.

Group 1

ticket, pickles, crackers

Which letter is silent? _____

Group 2

scenic, scentless, scissors

Which letter is silent? _____

Group 3

knickknack, knowledge, knotted

Which letter is silent? _____

Group 4

delightful, eyesight, frightening

Which letters are silent? _____

Then, write a story about a visit to the zoo. In your story, use at least two words from each group of sounds, or use silent consonant words that you find yourself.

Word Structure • *Challenge Activities*

Name _____ Date _____

Selection Vocabulary

Focus Having fun with words is a wonderful way to learn new vocabulary.

Apply **Make a Word Drawing Dictionary. Use the vocabulary words below, and change each word into a drawing. For example, for the word *waded*, you might put a bird's legs on the two *d*'s, and draw water around the legs. Use a separate sheet of paper for each word drawing. Under each word drawing, write the word and the definition.**

voyage	tide	sheltered	ripples
eroding	acres	claim	toppled

When you finish, put all of your pages together to make a dictionary. Share your drawings with a partner.

Name _____ Date _____

Cause and Effect

Focus Understanding the causes and the effects of events helps good readers understand what they read.

The **cause** is *why* something happened. The **effect** is *what* happened.

Apply **Read the nursery rhyme below. On a separate sheet of paper, answer the questions that follow the rhyme.**

[Line 1] For want of a nail the shoe was lost.

[Line 2] For want of a shoe the horse was lost.

[Line 3] For want of a horse the rider was lost.

[Line 4] For want of a rider the battle was lost.

[Line 5] For want of a battle the kingdom was lost.

[Line 6] And all for the want of a horseshoe nail.

1. What do the words "for want of" mean in the rhyme? What words might you use instead to make the rhyme easier to understand?

2. What kind of "shoe" does the rhyme mean?

3. Why did the horse lose its shoe?

4. Explain what happens in the first five lines of the rhyme. Write about each line by itself. In each line, tell the cause and the effect.

5. Does the sixth line of the poem identify a cause or an effect?

Comprehension Skill • *Challenge Activities*

Name _____ Date _____

Spelling

Focus A **word family** is a group of words that all share the same base word. Knowing the meaning of the base word can help you understand the meaning of the words in the word family.

Apply Identify the base words from the clues below. Write your answers on a separate sheet of paper. Under each base word, write the other words in the word family.

1. The base word has a silent consonant. The base word contains two vowels, and they are both the same.

2. The base word has a silent consonant. The base word contains two vowels, but they are both different.

3. The base word has a silent consonant. The base word contains one vowel.

4. The base word has a silent *e.*

5. The base word has a consonant blend.

live	living	honest	director	doubt
lively	honor	honesty	direction	doubtful
relive	honorable	direct	indirect	undoubted

Challenge words: know   unknown   knowledge

Choose two different words from the box and write clues for a partner. Trade clues with your partner, and see if you can guess each other's words.

Name _____ Date _____

Irregular Verb Tenses

Focus Finding regular patterns makes reading easier. **Irregular verbs** do not follow a regular verb pattern.

You must memorize irregular verbs to learn them.

Apply **Work with a partner. Write the following words on index cards—one word on each card.**

am	are	begin	bite	come	do
eat	give	go	grow	has	lose
run	see	stand	take	tell	write

Take turns picking cards. Look at the word, and tell your partner what consonants or vowels you need to change to form the past tense. Then, write the past tense verb on the index card. Answer the questions below.

• To make the past tense, one word needed all new letters. What was the word?

• To make the past tense, one word did not need any new letters. What was the word?

• To make the past tense, one word needed a new consonant, but it did not need a new vowel. What was the word?

• How are the past tenses of *stand* and *take* alike?

Review of Prefixes; Affixes as Syllables

Focus

An **affix** changes the meaning of a base word. Remember that a **prefix** is an affix that you add to the beginning of a word. A **suffix** is an affix that you add to the end of a word.

Apply

Work with a partner. Use a sheet of notebook paper to make eight boxes. Number the boxes from 1 to 8. Cut out each numbered box. Put the numbered boxes in a paper bag or other container so you cannot see them.

Take turns pulling out the numbered boxes. Match your number to the prefix In the list below.

1. *re-*   **2.** *un-*   **3.** *pre-*   **4.** *mis-*

5. *bi-*   **6.** *mid-*   **7.** *dis-*   **8.** *auto-*

With your partner, think of two words that begin with that prefix, and write a sentence using each word. Continue picking numbers and writing sentences until you have picked all the prefixes.

How many syllables does each base word have? How many syllables does each word have after you add the prefix? What would happen to the number of syllables if you added a suffix?

Name _____ Date _____

Word Families and Multisyllabic Words with Silent Consonants

Focus

Good readers know that the words in a **word family** all have the same *base* word.

Some words contain **silent consonants,** like the word *know.* The more you practice using the words, the more easily you will be able to read them.

Copy the words below onto a separate sheet of paper. Leave space around each word. Underline all of the silent consonants in each word. Next to each word, write the number of syllables in the word.

brighten	necktie	design	fasten
knit	mightily	knowing	whistle

Each word above is part of a word family. Find at least two more words that are part of the same family.

What happens to the number of syllables when you add or remove an affix to make a new word in the word family? When you divide the words into syllables, how would you divide a silent consonant?

Combine answers with other students to make larger word families.

Word Structure • *Challenge Activities*

Name _____ Date _____

Selection Vocabulary

Focus The more words you learn, the better you can understand what you read. If you are not sure what a word means, reread the story to see how it was used, or look it up in the dictionary.

Apply You are the food critic for your local newspaper. As a food critic, you go to a restaurant and order a meal. You decide what is good or bad about the food and the restaurant.

Write a review of a restaurant using the following vocabulary words. Tell your readers about the food, the service, and the atmosphere. Make up a restaurant, or write about your favorite or least favorite restaurant.

seasonal	produce	particular
necessities	featuring	discount

Keep these questions in mind when you are writing:

What is the name of the restaurant?

What kind of food does the restaurant serve?

What foods did you order? Is the restaurant clean?

Is the food expensive? Did the server bring the food quickly?

Are there coupons you can use to help pay for the meal?

When you finish, share your review with your teacher.

Challenge Activities • Vocabulary

Name _____ Date _____

Main Ideas and Supporting Details

Focus Readers can better understand what they read if they can identify the main idea and the supporting details. A **main idea** is what a paragraph or story is mostly about. **Supporting details** are facts, reasons, or ideas that add to or clarify the main idea.

Apply **Choose a topic below that you would like to write about.**

The Sears Tower   My Family Reunion

The Washington Monument   My Favorite Vacation

The Statue of Liberty   The Solar System

The Best Pet   The White House

On a separate sheet of paper, write a paragraph about the idea you chose. Underline the topic sentence.

Add supporting details about your topic to your paragraph. You will need to do research to find supporting details.

Keep in mind that a good topic sentence clearly states the main idea. Often the topic sentence is at the beginning of a paragraph. Sometimes it appears later in the paragraph.

When you finish, share your paragraph with a partner.

Comprehension Skill • *Challenge Activities*

Name _____ Date _____

Spelling

Focus This lesson reviews words with **prefixes, affixes** that change word meaning, and **word families**.

Apply You are a sports announcer on TV. You are ready to announce a race, which is just about to begin. On a separate sheet of paper, describe what happens. Write your description like a part in a play, as if you were saying it out loud. Use at least ten of the words below in your description. Try to include the challenge words *misspell* and *knowledge.*

mismatch	bicycle	restful	director	distrust
preview	doubtful	direct	indirect	unfair
movement	restless	direction	autopilot	midsummer

Challenge words: misspell   knowledge

Practice your announcing, and then announce the race to a partner. You can read what you have to say, rather than having to memorize it.

Name _____ Date _____

Complex Sentences

Focus **Complex sentences** make writing more interesting. A complex sentence is formed when a complete sentence is combined with an incomplete sentence. A complete sentence is called an **independent clause.** An incomplete sentence is called a **dependent clause.**

Both independent and dependent clauses have a subject and a verb. The only way for the dependent clause to make sense is to join it with the independent clause.

Apply **Turn the simple sentences below into complex sentences by adding a subordinate conjunction and joining the two sentences. Subordinate conjunctions include** *after, although, as, because, before, if, since, when, where, while, until,* **and** *unless.*

Write the complex sentences on a separate sheet of paper. Have fun!

1. We need to pack a picnic lunch. We go.

2. It snows. Let's go sledding.

3. Summer is here. I love to read under the tree by the library.

4. Ted can come. We can't play baseball.

5. I use my umbrella. It rains.

In each pair of sentences that you joined, which simple sentence became the dependent clause? Underline the dependent clause.

Name _____ **Date** _____

Antonyms, Synonyms, and Compound Words

Focus   **Antonyms** are words that mean the opposite, or nearly the opposite, of each other.

Synonyms are words that mean the same, or nearly the same, as each other.

Compound words are words made by combining two smaller words.

Apply   **Play the Triple Game. Answer the questions below. Use a separate sheet of paper for your answers.**

If you are not sure about the meaning of some of the words, use a dictionary to help you.

everybody	grandfather	nearby	nothing
farewell	myself	nighttime	overcast

1. For each word above, find an antonym.

2. For each word above, find a synonym.

3. Which words are compound words? Which synonyms are compound words? Separate every compound word into its word parts.

Name _____ Date _____

Contractions and Related Words

Focus

Contractions are two words combined together with an apostrophe (') in the place of the letters taken out.

Related words are words that have a common theme.

Apply

Read the words below. On a separate sheet of paper, change the words into contractions.

I am	I will	it is	you will	we are	he will
you are	we will	they are	they will	cannot	I have
could not	you have	do not	she has	does not	we have
should not	they have	would not	let us		

How are the words in each group below related? Write your answers on a separate sheet of paper. Add two more words to each group.

1. leaf   branch   trunk

2. page   word   chapter

3. feet   tail   trunk

4. tires   horn   windshield

Choose a group of related words. Write a short story using at least three of the words in the group. In your story, also use at least three contractions. Illustrate your story.

Display your work in your classroom.

Word Structure • *Challenge Activities*

Name _____ Date _____

Selection Vocabulary

Focus There are many different ways to learn new words. One way is to draw pictures about them.

Apply Divide up the following descriptions with a partner. Make four cartoons each. Use a separate sheet of drawing paper to illustrate each description.

Remember that a cartoon does not have to be funny. It is just a simple kind of drawing. Write a caption for each of your cartoons. Be sure to use the vocabulary word in your caption.

taking *gulps* of a drink

sleeping on a *cot*

an animal that is *howling*

lap up milk

a sun that is *setting*

something you might want to *borrow*

eager to do something

opening a *package*

When you finish, combine your cartoons into a book. Make a front and a back cover for your book. Display your book in your classroom.

Name _____ Date _____

Spelling

Focus This lesson reviews **long vowel** sound/spellings, **/j/, /s/, /n/, /r/, /f/, m/, consonant blends, compound words, related words,** and **contractions.**

Apply Your class volunteered to help out at the zoo for one day. You were assigned to work with the baby animals in the nursery. Write two paragraphs that tell how you spent the day. Use at least ten of the words below. Try to use the challenge words *eager, package,* and *wristband.*

strange	concert	peanut	washcloth	mute
these	wrap	didn't	pupil	limb
jacket	scarf	orphan	knuckle	you're

Challenge words: eager package wristband

Draw a picture to illustrate your writing.

Spelling • *Challenge Activities*

Name _____   Date _____

Unit 1 Review

Focus   **Verbs** show the action, condition, or state of being of the subject of a sentence. **State-of-being verbs** include *are, am,* and *is.*

Verb phrases are one or more helping verbs followed by the main verb.

A **simple subject** is the main word or group of words in a sentence. A **simple predicate** tells one thing about the subject. A **simple sentence** has one simple subject and one simple predicate.

Apply   You are going on a word safari. You are going to hunt words, phrases, and sentences. Choose an animal from the list below. Find a magazine article or book that tells you about the animal.

lion   rhinoceros   zebra   elephant   giraffe   hippopotamus

1. Choose two sentences with verb phrases. Write the sentences on a separate sheet of paper. Underline verb phrases.

2. Then, write two sentences. Underline the subjects and circle the predicates.

3. Find two complete simple sentences. Write your examples on your paper. Underline the subjects, and circle the verbs.

Name _____ Date _____

Regular and Irregular Plural Nouns

Focus

Most **plural nouns** are regular nouns. There are rules that explain how to form them. The most common way to form a plural noun is to add the letter s to the end of a word.

There are no rules for forming nouns with **irregular** endings. Good readers just have to study them until they know them.

Apply

Work with a partner. Write each word below on an index card.

goose	mouse	tooth	hand	wish	person
cow	house	friendship	foot	goldfish	woman

Stack the cards with the words facing down. Use a timer. Take turns picking cards. As soon as you choose a card, have your partner start the timer.

Look at the card, and say either "regular plural" or "irregular plural." Then, give the plural form, and use it in a sentence. Your partner should call time after forty-five seconds. If you cannot complete your answer within the time limit, work together to figure out the answer.

Word Structure • *Challenge Activities*

Name _____ Date _____

Homophones and Homographs

Focus **Homophones** are words that sound alike but have different meanings and are spelled differently. **Homographs** are words that are spelled the same but have different meanings.

Apply Read the two groups of words below. One group of words consists of homographs and the other of homophones. Fill in the correct title, either *homographs* or *homophones,* for each group of words.

Title: _____   Title: _____

plain	know	light	roll
eye	steal	nickel	story
heal	towed	spring	right
mist	flour	sink	left
piece	hour	mouse	glass

Choose five homographs and five homophones from the list. Write two sentences for each word. Show the different meanings of each word in your sentences.

Name _____ Date _____

Selection Vocabulary

Focus A crossword puzzle is a fun way to learn new vocabulary words.

Apply Use the selection vocabulary words from the story "Storm in the Night" to complete the puzzle.

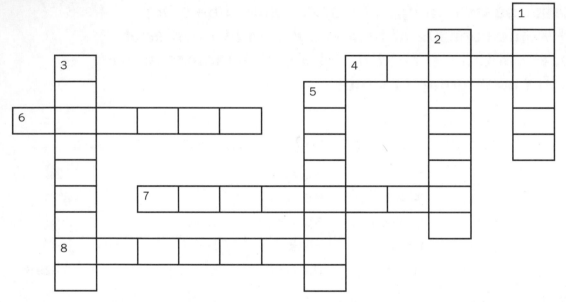

Across

4. The _____ on the police car was getting louder.

6. My mother asked me to do an _____ for her.

7. You feel proud when you _____ a fear.

8. When you are tired, it is _____ to want to rest awhile.

Down

1. Grandmother lit the candle that was on the _____ above the fireplace.

2. It rained so hard we were _____.

3. The milk spilled and went _____ over the side of the table.

5. The thunder was so loud we could _____ hear the actors in the play.

Vocabulary • *Challenge Activities*

Name _____ **Date** _____

Spelling

Focus This lesson reviews **homophones, homographs, long vowel sounds, /ōō/, plurals,** and **irregular plurals.**

Apply There was a robbery at a jewelry store. You are a detective on the police force, and you have just found the missing jewels. Now you have to write up a report telling how you found them. Write a report on a separate sheet of paper, and use at least ten of the words in the box below. Try to include the challenge words *statue, hyena,* and *swallow.*

they're	there	geese	moose	cue
train	owner	throat	steel	weighty
cries	bright	rubies	lead	steal

Challenge words: statue   hyena   swallow

Trade reports with a partner to see how your partner solved the crime.

Name _____ Date _____

Units 1 and 2 Review

Focus You already learned about using **quotation marks,** commas in quotations, and commas in **series.** You also know about **capitalization, possessive nouns and pronouns,** and **regular** and **irregular plural nouns.** Practice, because it helps you remember what you have learned.

Apply George interviewed Glenda for the school newspaper. Here is a draft of the interview. Find the mistakes, and correct them. When you finish, circle the possessive pronouns. Underline any regular plural nouns in red. Underline any irregular plural nouns in blue.

What is your favorite book? George asked.

Glenda answered, My favorite book is ramona by beverly cLEARY. She and her sister remind me of me and my sister."

"Good," George said. Then he asked "What are your favorite foods?"

I like peaches strawberries and walnuts a lot" glenda answered.

What is your favorite thing to do in the summer? George asked next.

Glenda said Last summer I went to chicago with my family. We all piled into my aunts car to go there. we had such fun in Chicago! we took an elevator up one of the tallest buildings in the world. It is called the sears tower. We were more than 1,350 feet above the ground. the men and women below looked like little ants! my favorite thing, though, is to go swimming in the summer. I think it is my sisters favorite thing too."

When you finish, share your answers with your teacher.

Grammar, Usage, and Mechanics • *Challenge Activities*

Name _____ Date _____

Inflectional Endings *-ed* and *-ing*

Focus | **Inflectional endings** change the tense of a base verb. When you add the ending **-ed** to a base verb, it changes the verb to the past tense. When you add the ending **-ing** to a base verb, the verb shows continuous action, or present tense.

Remember these two rules:

- When adding **-ed** to a base verb that ends in e, drop the e and then add *-ed.*

- When adding **-ing** to a base verb that ends in e, drop the e and then add *-ing.*

Apply | **Choose your words from the list of base verbs in the box below. On a separate sheet of paper, change the endings by adding** *-ed* **or** *-ing.*

Write a letter to a friend or a family member telling them about your life. Include details about what you do at school and at home. Use at least eight of the words you make in your letter.

call	dust	go	hitch	load	
pick	slice	smell	use	write	bake

When you finish, read the letter to your family.

Name _____ **Date** _____

Comparative and Superlative Adjectives

Focus **Adjectives** are words that add information to a noun or pronoun. **Comparative adjectives** compare two things, people, places, or ideas. **Superlative adjectives** compare *more* than two things, people, places, or ideas.

Read the story below. Underline the regular adjectives. Circle the comparative adjectives. Put two lines under the superlative adjectives.

Mrs. Reno wrote this problem on the board:

John is taller than Billy. James is shorter than Billy. Who is the shortest?

Sammy looked at the problem. "Oh, no! This is even harder than the one yesterday," Sammy moaned.

"It is a hard problem, Sammy, but I know you can figure it out. You have figured out harder problems before," Mrs. Reno said with a small smile.

Sammy studied the problem. He drew diagrams.

"This problem is more enjoyable than I first thought," he said to himself. "In fact it is the most enjoyable problem I've ever done. This is the best day ever!"

Then, on a separate sheet of paper, list the irregular comparative and superlative adjectives. Can you solve the problem on the board? Who is the shortest?

Word Structure • *Challenge Activities*

Name _____ Date _____

Selection Vocabulary

Focus When you use words that you have just learned, it helps you remember their meanings.

Apply **Each of the ideas below contains one of the vocabulary words from "Pueblo Storyteller." Choose two of the ideas from the list. Write one or two paragraphs for each idea you choose. For each idea, be sure to include the vocabulary word in your writing.**

- Do research about pueblos. Describe and illustrate a pueblo.

- Describe a car or a plane that has a modern design. Draw a picture of the car or plane.

- Describe some family traditions. If you can, illustrate your description.

- Write about some of your ancestors.

- Draw an object shaped like a cylinder. Describe it.

When you finish, share your writing and drawings with your teacher.

Name _____   Date _____

Drawing Conclusions

Focus People use information from what they read or what they see to **draw conclusions** about a character, an event, or information that is not stated directly. A conclusion must be supported by details in the text.

Apply **Read the following paragraphs, and answer the questions at the end of each paragraph. Write your answers on a separate sheet of paper.**

Rosita had a magnet. She knew that magnets would stick to things that were made of iron. She held her magnet next to a paper clip. The paper clip stuck to the magnet. She held her magnet next to a toy car. It stuck to the toy car. She held her magnet next to a piece of paper, but the paper fell to the floor.

What conclusions can you draw? Give reasons for your answer. Think of two more details that could support your conclusion.

Cal and his brother went to a movie. Cal's mother and aunt went to see a different movie. Cal and his brother were laughing as they walked out of the movie. Cal's mother and aunt were wiping tears from their eyes as they walked out of their movie.

What conclusions can you draw? Give reasons for your answer. Think of two more details that could support your conclusion.

When you finish, trade papers with a partner. Compare the details you each thought of.

Name _____ Date _____

Spelling

Copyright © SRA/McGraw-Hill. Permission is granted to reproduce this page for classroom use.

Focus This lesson reviews /**oo**/ spelled *oo*, /$\overline{oo}$/ spelled *oo*, /**aw**/, /**ow**/, /**oi**/, **inflectional endings,** and **comparative** and **superlative adjectives.**

Apply Use each word in the box below to create a question. For example, suppose you choose the word *cuter*. You might ask the question, "Which animal do you think is cuter, a kitten or a puppy?" Write your questions on a separate sheet of paper. Underline the spelling word in each question.

foot	prowl	bounce	walk	thought
departing	more	cuter	stall	soon
stumbled	hoist	greatest	pure	vault

Challenge words: uniform   haughty

Find a partner, and take turns asking each other and answering the questions you each wrote.

Name _____ Date _____

Unit 2 Review

Focus Four types of sentences are **declarative, interrogative, imperative,** and **exclamatory.** You use each type of sentence for a different reason.

The subject of a sentence is a **noun.** Sometimes a noun is also used as a direct object. Wherever a noun is used, you can use a **pronoun** instead.

Apply **Work with a partner to help make a cookbook. Describe how to make a salad, a pizza, a taco, or your favorite kind of dish.**

In your description, use at least one declarative sentence, one interrogative sentence, one imperative sentence, and one exclamatory sentence. Also include at least two direct objects and two pronouns. Try to use one pronoun as a subject and one as a direct object.

When you finish, combine your work with those of other teams to make a group cookbook.

Name _____ Date _____

Suffixes *-ly, -y, -ment, -tion, -ful,* and *-able*

Focus

The meaning of a base word changes when a **suffix** is added. Some suffixes change the base word into an **adjective.** Some suffixes change the base word into an **adverb.**

Apply

Next Wednesday is National Suffix Day. You and your partner have been asked to design billboards for the celebration using the suffixes *-ly, -y, -ment, -tion, -ful,* and *-able.* The Billboard Commission will choose two billboards to put up in your area.

Here are the rules from the Billboard Commission:

- Each billboard will present three different suffixes.
- Each billboard must explain what the suffixes mean.
- Each billboard must present a sentence that uses a word with each suffix.
- Each billboard must say whether the word with the suffix is an adjective or an adverb.

You and your partner have decided to split up the work. Each of you will prepare plans for a billboard.

When you are satisfied with your plan, make a poster. Display your posters in your classroom.

Name _____ Date _____

Suffixes *-ity, -less, -ness,* and *-sion;* Greek and Latin Roots

Focus Many different things affect the meaning of words. Base words change when a **suffix** is added. Words that have **Latin** and **Greek roots** come from words that people spoke in ancient Rome and Greece. If you know what the roots mean, you can better understand the meanings of words.

Apply **You are in the Word Olympics! You can earn a silver medal *and* a gold medal! However, you have to earn them in order, first the silver and then the gold medal.**

Earn a silver medal. **On a separate sheet of paper, write one word that ends with each of the suffixes *-ity, -less, -ness,* and *-sion.* Explain what each of these suffixes means.**

Earn a gold medal. **On a separate sheet of paper, write four words that have four different Greek roots. Underline the root, and tell what the root means.**

On a separate sheet of paper, write four words that have four different Latin roots. Underline the root and tell what the root means.

When you finish, design a gold medal that says "Word Parts Champion." You can add other words if you like. Design the front and the back of the medal. Display your work and your medal in your classroom.

Word Structure • *Challenge Activities*

Name _____ Date _____

Selection Vocabulary

 **Focus** Good readers play word games to practice using new vocabulary words.

 **Apply** **Work with a partner. Write one word on each index card.**

stored	cleared	survived	boasted
exhausted	affectionately	exaggerated	claim

Stack the cards, and place them on the table so you cannot see the words. Take turns picking cards. Look at the word, and give clues to your partner. Your partner has to guess the word. You can give word clues, or you can act out the words.

When you finish, study the words. Which words have suffixes? Can you identify the base words?

Name _____   Date _____

Author's Point of View

Focus The **author's point of view** refers to the way the author tells a story.

Sometimes an author tells a story as if the storyteller were a character in the story. This kind of storytelling is called a **first-person narrative.** The words *I, me, mine, my, we, our,* and *ours* are clue words used in a first-person narrative.

Another way to tell a story is from the point of view of someone who is not in the story. A story with this kind of viewpoint is called a **third-person narrative.** Stories told from the point of view of a "third person" use clue words such as *he, him, she, her, they,* and *theirs.*

Apply There is a forest fire. *You are a firefighter.* **Write a short paragraph describing what it is like to fight the big forest fire. Explain how you got to the fire. Describe what you saw and what it was like. Explain how you feel.**

You are a reporter for the newspaper. **Write a short paragraph describing to your readers what is happening. Explain how the fire started and what the firefighters are doing. Explain what the fire looks like and what the weather is like.**

Which report did you write in the first person? Which did you write in the third person? Underline the words in each paragraph that show the author's point of view.

Comprehension Skill • *Challenge Activities*

Name _____ Date _____

Spelling

Focus The suffixes **-ly -y, -ment, -ful, -able, -ity, -less, -ness,** and **-sion** can be added to the end of a word to change the meaning of the word.

When the inflectional ending **-ing** is added to a base verb, it shows that the action is happening now. The inflectional ending **-ed** shows that the action happened in the past.

Some words have **Latin** and **Greek roots.**

Apply You are the judge in an art show. You are going to give a speech to announce the first and second prize winners. On a separate sheet of paper, write your speech. Your speech should describe what each of the two pieces of art looks like. Use at least nine words from the list below. Try to include the challenge words *affectionately, exaggerated,* and *exhausted.*

astronomer	support	graphic	flawless	congratulate
quality	geologist	neatly	basement	shyness
invasion	padded	painting	bendable	colorful

Challenge words: affectionately   exaggerated   exhausted

Practice giving your speech. Then, give your speech to a classmate. You can read your speech. You do not have to memorize it.

Name _____ Date _____

Units 3 and 4 Review

Focus When you practice what you learn, it helps you remember all that you have learned.

Apply **Play the Suppose Game. Write your answers on a separate sheet of paper.**

1. *Suppose* you have to combine these two sentences into a compound sentence. How would you do it? Is there another way?

Ellie came home. Mother greeted her at the door.

2. *Suppose* you have to add periods and commas to the sentences below. Where would you add them?

My aunt and I are going to visit Mrs Allen She is going to give us one red fish one blue fish and one yellow fish

3. *Suppose* you have to underline the compound subjects and circle the compound predicates in the sentences below. Which parts would you underline and circle?

In the summer, my sister and I always go on picnics.

In the winter, I go skating and make snow angels.

4. *Suppose* you have to underline compound words. Which of the following words would you underline?

woodwork   schoolhouse   table   summertime   armchair   lightning

5. *Suppose* you have to change four words into contractions. What words would you choose? How would you change them?

Grammar, Usage, and Mechanics • *Challenge Activities*

Name _____ Date _____

Prefixes *re-, un-, pre-, mis-, bi-, mid-, dis-,* and *auto-*

**Focus**

Prefixes are affixes that you add to the beginning of a base word. Prefixes change the meaning of the word. Sometimes prefixes are a shorter way of saying something. For example, instead of saying, "Let's glue the door again," you can say, "Let's *reglue* the door."

Apply

Work with a partner. Write these prefixes on square pieces of paper, one prefix to a square.

| re- | pre- | bi- | dis- |
| un- | mis- | mid- | auto- |

1. Fold the papers in half so you cannot see the prefixes. Then, drop all the papers in a bag or hat.

2. Take turns pulling a paper from the bag. Read the prefix out loud, say what it means, and write a word with the prefix on a sheet of paper.

3. When you are done picking all the prefixes, work with your partner to list at least three more words for each prefix.

When you finish, share your lists with your teacher.

Name _____ Date _____

Affixes; Word Families; Multisyllabic Words with Silent Consonants

Focus You have learned much about **affixes, word families,** and **words with more than one syllable** and **silent consonants.** Now is your chance to show a bit of what you learned.

Apply **You are a detective. You have been asked to find out certain things about affixes. Note your answers on a separate sheet of paper as you go along.**

1. You have just stumbled on these words:

   reread   handy   unfold   joyful   disappear   friendly

   Can you detect the base words? For each base word, how does the affix change the meaning of the word? What happens to the number of syllables in a word when an affix is added to the word?

2. Aha! You have discovered this grouping of words below. Are they related? How? What do you call this kind of word grouping? What is the root word?

   wash; washing; unwashed; rewash; washable; washer

3. Your final instruction is to divide the words below into syllables and to find the silent consonants. Rewrite each word on your sheet of paper. After you divide the words into syllables, underline the silent consonants.

   answer   wrinkled   headlight   itching   flicker   island

Word Structure • *Challenge Activities*

Name _____ Date _____

Selection Vocabulary

Focus When you read, you learn new words. The more you use the new words, the better you understand their meanings.

Last night there was a terrible storm. When you got up this morning, you looked all around you to see the damage the storm caused.

Write about the storm in your journal. Use at least four of the words in the following list. Write at least two paragraphs. Illustrate a sentence or two from your journal.

deny
common
shingle
battered
gust
huddled
haste
calculate

Read your journal entry to your class, and display your journal page.

Name _____ Date _____

Compare and Contrast

Focus
When you **compare** things, you find out how they are alike.

When you **contrast** things, you find out how they are different.

You can compare and contrast ideas, thoughts, objects, places, animals, and people. You become an excellent observer and thinker when you use comparing and contrasting skills.

Apply
You are going to the zoo. At the zoo, you visit the lions. You think about how much they remind you of your pet cat, Fluffy.

When you get home, you decide to write a compare-and-contrast book about the lions at the zoo and Fluffy. In your book, write at least three ways that Fluffy and the lions are alike. Show at least three ways they are different. Illustrate your book with your own drawings or with pictures from magazines or old calendars.

When you finish, compare and contrast your book with another classmate's book.

Comprehension Skill • *Challenge Activities*

Name _____ Date _____

Spelling

Focus The spelling words in this lesson review the prefixes *re-, un-, pre-, mis-, bi-, mid-,* and *dis-,* word families, /n/, /r/, /j/, and **affixes** that change word meaning.

Apply Mrs. Webster is writing a list of words for a new dictionary. When she printed out her list, she saw that something went wrong. The last letter of each word was missing. All the last letters ended up in a row at the bottom of the list. She needs your help. She would like you to copy the words in the box below and add the missing letters.

beautifu	bicep	dislik	fina	finis
finit	homeles	huddle	judg	knac
midnigh	mistrea	nonfictio	precoo	rewrit
scener	unwra	wrec		

Letters: d e e e e h ll k k k n p s s tt y

When you are done, choose two words. Write each word, and then write a definition of the word. Add your words to a class dictionary.

Name _____ Date _____

Unit 4 Review

 **Focus** You learned about **adverbs, synonyms,** and **antonyms.** You learned also about **subject** and **verb agreement** and about **verb tenses.** Knowing all these things makes you a better reader and a better writer.

Apply Write your answers on a separate sheet of paper.

Adverb? **In the following sentence, identify the adverbs. Tell what the adverb modifies.**

Anita wore a brightly colored ribbon in her long, dark hair.

Synonym and Antonym! **Give a synonym *and* an antonym for each of the following words.**

begin   little   outdoors   receive   remain   vanish

Subject and Verb Tense Agreement? **Rewrite the sentences below with the correct verb tense and subject/verb agreement.**

I *cooks* dinner every Friday night. Last night is Thursday, so Odelia *cook* dinner. Next Saturday night, Leo *cooked* dinner.

Answer Key

Lesson 3

page 16
Spelling
haven't
wasn't
aren't
doesn't
moment
o'clock
shouldn't

Lesson 4

Page 19
Word Structure
The jem family *or* jewel family
Things found at a baseball game
Drinks, *or* liquids

Page 20
Vocabulary
1. splendor
2. mercy
3. sighed
4. magnificent
5. clung
6. timidly
7. despair
8. flattered

Lesson 5

Page 23
Phonics
amaze
(badge)
(best)
chief

explain
(fancy)
(gentle)
(giant)
honey
kite
leaves
lonely
(pencil)
plate
player
(speedy)
(stone)
(strange)

Lesson 5

Page 27
Spelling
knot
write
phony
climb
knee
graph
phase
know
wreath
thumb
wrist
lamb
trophy
knife
comb
triumph

Answer Key

Lesson 1

Page 33
GUM
her coat
book's cover
puppies' tails
your idea
umbrella's handle
children's game
families' houses
Tom's bike
bird's beak
Their shoes

Lesson 2

Page 34
Phonics
slow
throw
show
below
road
boat
grow
glow

Page 38
Spelling
/ō/
toast
coach
throw
roast
crow
oatmeal
loan

grow
float
pillow
/ī/
mice
cacti
/ē/
deer
teeth
No Long Vowels
women
oxen
fish
Irregular Plurals
deer
teeth
cacti
mice
oxen
women
fish

Lesson 4

Page 47
Word Structure
two
see
weak
wood
meat
their
eye
pale
reed
right
ewe

Answer Key

two/to

see/sea

weak/week

wood/would

meat/meet

their/there

eye/I

pale/pail

reed/read

right/write

ewe/you

Page 49

meat/meet

tail/tale

tow/toe

seem/seam

piece/peace

grown/groan

by/buy

hoarse/horse

waist/waste

hoarse/horse

Answer Key

Lesson 3

Page 72
Spelling
f<u>a</u>ll
c<u>au</u>ght
f<u>a</u>st<u>er</u>
<u>A</u>ugust
t<u>a</u>lk
sm<u>a</u>ll
f<u>au</u>ght
<u>ya</u>wn
b<u>ou</u>ght
th<u>i</u>nn<u>e</u>st
h<u>a</u>wk
t<u>au</u>ght
ch<u>a</u>lk
t<u>a</u>ller
<u>au</u>t<u>o</u>
squ<u>a</u>wk
h<u>a</u>pp<u>ie</u>r

Lesson 4

Page 74
Phonics
annoy
asteroid
avoid
boil
boy
choice
destroy
employ
enjoy
join

joint
joy
noise
oyster
point
poise
spoil
toil
toy
voice
void
voyage
voice
void
boil
coin
joint
appoint
noise
oyster
moist

Page 75
Word Structure
better/best
less/least
more/most
worse/worst

Page 78
GUM
1. As tall as <u>a</u> giraffe
2. As strong as <u>an</u> ox
3. As hot as <u>an</u> oven
4. As welcome as <u>a</u> skunk

Answer Key • *Challenge Activities*

Answer Key

Lesson 1

Page 84
Word Structure
gently
icy
gladly
cheerfully
warmly
misty
noisy
helpfully
rainy
messy
scary
sleepy
immediately
slowly
snowy

Page 85
Word Structure
enjoyment
celebration
entertainment
detection
movement
government
invention
action
involvement
attraction

Page 88
Spelling
action
invention
selection

statement [no change]
treatment
chewy
payment
apartment
scary
slightly
easily
kindly
partly
shipment
daily
rusty [no change]
bony

Page 89
GUM
an apple, a peach, and a pear
Yes, I find them
a cracker, some cheese, and an olive.
No, I'm too full.

Lesson 2

Page 95
GUM
1. anyone
   somebody
   everywhere
   nothing
2. body
   some
   one
   no

Answer Key

3. I'm
you're
haven't
4. is not
could not
you will

Lesson 3

Page 98
Vocabulary

| New Moon | Waxing Crescent | First Quarter | Full Moon | Waning Crescent | Last Quarter |

Lesson 4

Page 104
Vocabulary

1. The word part *naut* means "ship" or "navel." The root *naut* comes from Latin *nauticus,* which comes from the Greek word *nautikos,* from *nautēs* "sailor," or from *naus* "ship."
Astronaut: a person who travels beyond the earth's atmosphere; *also*: a trainee for spaceflight

2. *Gigantic* comes from the Greek word *gigantikos,* from the root *gigant-, gigas* or "giant."
Gigantic: exceeding the usual or expected (as in size, force, or prominence)

3. *Orbit* comes from the Latin *orbita* which means "path" or "rut."
Orbit: **a:** a path described by one body in its revolution about another (as by the earth about the sun or by an electron about an atomic nucleus); *also* : one complete revolution of a body describing such a path
b: a circular path

Page 106
GUM

word	synonym / antonym
bald	bare / hairy
difficult	hard / easy
freezing	cold / hot
near	close / far
noisy	loud / quiet
rapid	fast / slow
scream	shout / whisper
small	tiny / huge
terrible	awful / wonderful
toss	throw / catch
under	below / over
find	discover / lose

Lesson 5

Page 111
GUM

For "Rain":
cross out *are* and write *is*
cross out *fall* and write *falls*
cross out *They* and write *It*

For "The Lazy Roof":
cross out *have* and write *has*
cross out *has* and write *have*

For "A Walk in the Woods":
cross out *goes* and write *go*
cross out *say* and write *says;* cross out *are* and write *is;* cross out *sees* and write *see*
cross out *continues* and write *continue*

Answer Key

Lesson 1

Page 113
Word Structure
1. presweetened
2. mislay
3. predawn
4. misdate or miswrite or predate

Lesson 3

Page 123
Word Structure
"Suppose you had a <u>handful</u> of coins, and you <u>dropped</u> one as you went to the store. What would you do?" Frankie <u>asked</u>.
"I would <u>retrace</u> my steps to find it," <u>answered</u> Grandmother <u>promptly</u>.
"But suppose it was a <u>windy</u>, <u>freezing</u> day. Would you take the same <u>action</u>?" he <u>asked</u>.
"Hmmm," Grandmother said. "I would <u>rethink</u> my plan and look <u>carefully</u> on the way back."

hand ⬚ful⬚
dropp⬚ed⬚
⬚re⬚ trace
an swer⬚ed⬚
prompt ⬚ly⬚
win d⬚y⬚
freez ⬚ing⬚
ac ⬚tion⬚
⬚re⬚ think
car ⬚ful⬚ ⬚ly⬚

Page 124
Word Structure
<u>Prefixes</u>
bimonthly

misplace
refill
retie
unopened
unplanned

<u>Suffixes</u>
beautiful
careless
doable
endless
hairless
hopeful
readable
thankful

Affixes:
-able means "not" or "to do the opposite of"
bi- means "two"
-ful means "full of"
-less means "without" or "not having"
mis- means "wrong" or "bad"
re- means "again"
un- means "not" or "to do the opposite of"
The affixes *un-* and *–less* make the base word its opposite.

Lesson 4

Page 129
Word Structure
act, action, actor, actress, active, enact, reenact, reenactment
animate, animation, animatedly, animated, animating, reanimate
breathe, breath, breathless, breathed breathing, inbreathe

Answer Key

build, building, rebuild, built, inbuilt, buildings
freeze, refreeze, unfreeze, frozen, froze
frighten, fright, frightened, frightening, frighteningly
joy, joyful, joyless, joylessly, joyfully, joylessness, enjoy, rejoice, enjoyable, rejoicing
live, living, lived, life, lifeless, alive, outlive, unlived
move, moving, moved, unmoved, unmoved, remove, unmoving,
snow, snowy, snowing, snowflake, snowball, snowbell, snowmelt, snowboard, snowman
try, trying, tried, retry, tries
write, rewrite, miswrite, writer, writing, written, wrote, writes, writ, skywrite, typewriter, handwrite, handwritten

Page 130
Word Structure
Group 1
tic   ket
pic   kles
crac   kers
The letter c is silent.
Group 2
sce   nic
scent   less
scis   sors
The letter c is silent.
Group 3
knick   knack
knowl   edge
knot   ted
The letter k is silent.
Group 4
de   light   ful
eye   sight

fright   en   ing
The letters *gh* are silent.
The letter *c* is silent in the word *knickknack*.

Page 131
Vocabulary
voyage *v.* to journey by water or through space
tide *n.* the rise and fall of the sea
sheltered *adj.* protected from danger
ripples *n.* plural form of **ripple:** a design created by waves
eroding *n.* the process of wearing or washing away slowly
acres *n.* plural form of **acre:** a measurement equal to 43,560 square feet
claim *v.* to take as one's own
toppled *v.* past tense of **topple:** to fall or make fall forward

Page 132
Comprehension
1. The words "for want of" means "because."
2. a horseshoe
3. either because a nail came loose and was lost or a replacement nail could not be found

4. | cause | effect |
|---|---|
| line 1: lost/missing nail | lost horseshoe |
| line 2: missing horseshoe | horse unable to ride to battle |
| line 3: no horse | no soldier |
| line 4: soldier missing from battle | battle lost |
| line 5: lost battle | kingdom taken over |

5. The sixth line identifies the cause (the lost nail).

Answer Key

Page 134
GUM

am	was
are	were
begin	began
bite	bit (did not need any new letters)
come	came
do	did
eat	ate
give	gave
go	went (needed all new letters)
grow	grew
has	had (added a consonant, no vowel change)
lose	lost
run	ran
see	saw
stand	stood
take	took
tell	told
write	wrote

"stood" and " took" are spelled with the letters oo

Lesson 5

Page 136
Word Structure

bri<u>gh</u>ten (2)	bright, brightness, brighter brightening, brightly
ne<u>c</u>ktie (2)	retie, untie, tie, ties, tying, tied, bowtie, untied
desi<u>g</u>n (2)	designer, redesign, designing, designedly
fas<u>t</u>en (2)	fastener, fast, fastening, fastened, unfasten, refasten
<u>k</u>nit (1)	knitted, knitter, knitting, reknit, unknit,
mi<u>gh</u>tily (3)	might, mighty, almighty, mightier, mightiest
<u>k</u>nowing (2)	know, knew, knowing, unknowingly, knowledge, knowable, unknowable, knowledgeable, knowledgably, knowingness
w<u>hi</u>s<u>t</u>le (2)	whistler, whistling, whistleable, pennywhistle, whistles

Answer Key

Lesson 1

Page 141
Word Structure

<u>word</u>	<u>antonym</u>	<u>synonym</u>	<u>compound</u>
everybody	nobody	everyone	every/body, no/body, every/one
farewell	hello	goodbye	fare/well, good/bye
grandfather		grandpa	grand/father
myself	yourself	me	my/self, your/self
nearby	far	close	near/by
nighttime	daytime	evening	night/time
nothing	something	zero	no/thing, some/thing
overcast	sunny	cloudy	over/cast

Page 142
Word Structure

I'm, I'll, it's, you'll, we're, he'll, you're, we'll, they're, they'll, can't
I've, couldn't, you've, don't, she's, doesn't, we've, shouldn't, they've, wouldn't, let's

1. words having to do with trees
2. words having to do with books
3. words having to do with elephants
4. words having to do with automobiles

Lesson 2

Page 146
Word Structure

<u>regular plural</u>	<u>irregular plural</u>
cow, cows	goose, geese
house, houses	mouse, mice
friendship, friendships	tooth, teeth
hand, hands	foot, feet
wish, wishes	goldfish, goldfish *or* goldfishes
	person, people
	woman, women

Page 147
Word Structure

Title: homophones
plain / plane
eye / I
heal / heel
mist / missed
piece/ peace
know / no
steal / steel
towed / toed
flour / flower
hour / our

Title: homographs
light
nickel
spring
sink
mouse
roll
story
right
left
glass

Answer Key • *Challenge Activities*

Answer Key

Page 148
Selection Vocabulary
   1 *Down:* mantel
   2 *Down:* drenched
   3 *Down:* streaming
   5 *Down:* scarcely
   4 *Across:* siren
   6 *Across:* errand
   7 *Across:* overcome
   8 *Across:* natural

Page 150
GUM
ᵛWhat is your favorite book?ᵛ George asked.

Glenda answered, ᵛMy favorite book is ramona by beverly cLEARY. She and her sister remind me of me and my sister."

"Good," George said. Then he asked, "What are your favorite foods?"

I like peaches, strawberries, and walnuts a lot," glenda answered.

ᵛWhat is your favorite thing to do in the summer?ᵛ George asked next.

Glenda said, ᵛLast summer I went to chicago with my family. We all piled into my aunt's car to go there. we had such fun in Chicago! we took an elevator up one of the tallest buildings in the world. It is called the sears tower. We were more than 1,350 feet above the ground. the men and women below looked like little ants! my favorite thing, though, is to go swimming in the summer.

I think it's my sister's favorite thing too."

Regular plural nouns; foods, peaches, strawberries, walnuts, buildings, ants
Irregular plural nouns; men, women

Lesson 3

Page 152
Word Structure
harder
hard; harder; small
more enjoyable; most enjoyable; best
Problem answer: James is the shortest

Lesson 4

Page 157
Word Structure
-*ment* means "action" or "process"
-*tion* means "action" or "process"
-*ful* means "full of"
-*able* means "able or tending to be"

Page 158
Word Structure
-*ity* means "state of being"
 -*less* means "without" or "not having"
-*ness* means "state of being"
-*sion* means "the action of"
ast means "star"
graph means "something written or drawn"
log (sometimes spelled *logue*) means "to speak"
scop means "to look at or examine"
grat means "thankful or pleasing"
mar means "sea or ocean"
miss (sometimes spelled *mit*) means "sent"
port means "carry"

UNIT 6

Answer Key

Page 162
GUM

2. My aunt and I are going to visit
   Mrs⊙Allen⊙She is going to give us one
   red fish∧ one blue fish∧ and one yellow
   fish⊙

3. In the summer, <u>my sister and I</u> always
   go on picnics.
   In the winter, I go skating and make
   snow angels.

4. <u>woodwork</u>; <u>schoolhouse</u>; <u>summertime</u>;
   <u>armchair</u>

Lesson 5

Page 164
Word Structure

1. word (# of   base word   meaning
   syllables)
   reread (2)   read (1)   to read again
   handy (2)   hand (1)   at hand
   unfold (2)   fold (1)   to open folds
   joyful (2)   joy (1)   full of joy
   disappear (3) appear (2)   to cease to
                               appear
   friendly (2)   friend (1)   in a manner of
                               a friend

2. This grouping is a word family. The root
   word is *wash*.

3. an s<u>w</u>er   <u>wr</u>in kled   head   li<u>gh</u>t
   i<u>tch</u> ing   fli<u>ck</u> er   <u>is</u> land

Page 168
GUM
Adverb?

brightly modifies *ribbon*

	Synonym	Antonym
begin	start	finish
little	small	big
outdoors	outside	inside
receive	take	give
remain	stay	go
vanish	disappear	appear

Subject and Verb Tense Agreement?

I <u>cook</u> dinner every Friday night. Last night
was Thursday, so Odelia <u>cooked</u> dinner. Next
Saturday night Leo <u>will cook</u> dinner.